DELIVERANCE
from
DEPRESSION

DELIVERANCE *from* DEPRESSION

FINDING HOPE AND HEALING THROUGH THE ATONEMENT OF CHRIST

G.G. VANDAGRIFF

GREG VANDAGRIFF

DAVID P. VANDAGRIFF

Covenant Communications, Inc.

Front cover © Shawn Gearhart, back cover © Graeme Purdy both courtesy of istockphoto.com

Cover design copyrighted 2008 by Covenant Communications, Inc.

Published by Covenant Communications, Inc.
American Fork, Utah

Printed in Canada
First Printing: August 2008

14 13 12 11 10 09 08   10 9 8 7 6 5 4 3 2 1

ISBN-13 978-1-59811-648-9
ISBN-10 1-59811-648-7

To our Lord and Savior Jesus Christ
in gratitude for His Atoning sacrifice.

ACKNOWLEDGMENTS

In gratitude to Judge Thomas B. Griffith, who led us in our discovery of the real power of the Atonement; Dr. Richard Holmes, who followed the Spirit in prescribing medications for us; Dr. Robert Williams, who counseled with all of us; Paula Nummela, who was G.G.'s visiting teacher during many of the years she was depressed; Zina Whetten, who was with G.G. through the worst and encouraged her to see a doctor; Greg's mission presidents: President Smith and President Browning of the Georgia Atlanta North Mission, and President Lund and President Methusak of the Georgia Atlanta Mission.

And I have been supported under trials and troubles of every kind, yea, and in all manner of afflictions; yea, God has delivered me from prison, and from bonds, and from death; yea, and I do put my trust in him, and he will still deliver me.

Alma 36:27

TABLE OF CONTENTS

INTRODUCTION

*And if it so be that the children of men keep the command-
ments of God he doth . . . strengthen them*—1 Nephi 17:3

We, the authors of this book, come to you with three unique
perspectives on clinical depression. This illness has touched each of our
lives in unique and profound ways. G.G. Vandagriff was first diagnosed
with depression after she gave birth to her second child. She then struggled with the illness for twenty-five years before she found healing.
Hers is a story of living with depression as a mother and wife. Gregory
Vandagriff, G.G.'s son, was diagnosed with depression when he was
thirteen and struggled under this burden for the next eight years. His is
a story of combating—and ultimately conquering—this illness as a
teenager and in his early twenties while in the mission field. David
Vandagriff, G.G.'s husband and Greg's father, tells a story of one not
afflicted by depression but nonetheless affected by it, as a father and
husband of loved ones suffering from depression. The healing he had
prayed for over many years finally came when David, then bishop of a
student singles ward, and G.G. began studying the power of the
Atonement in depth according to the wishes of the stake presidency.
David was counseled to have every talk and every lesson be explicitly
tied to the Atonement. The resulting experiences changed his and his
family's lives.

These are the experiences we wish to share with you. We bring
you our stories and perspectives, and most of all our testimony of the
Atonement of Jesus Christ, which has been the ultimate source of

the healing that has taken place in our lives. Our mission in writing this book is threefold:

1. To testify to all who suffer, be it from clinical depression or any other manner of affliction, that deliverance can be achieved through both the vertical and horizontal aspects of the Atonement. Through the experiences and miracles we've witnessed in our own lives, we have gained a stronger conviction that learning how to access the Savior's Atonement is one of the most fundamental purposes of our existence here on earth.
2. To offer hope and understanding to those suffering from clinical depression and PTSD (post-traumatic stress disorder) by sharing our own experiences with healing through both medical means and the power of the Atonement of Jesus Christ.
3. To help the family members, friends, and associates of individuals who suffer from clinical depression to gain understanding, learn how they can better cope with this illness, and discover how they can better aid their loved ones.

We are not so much authorities as witnesses that deliverance through the Atonement of Jesus Christ is possible. As we put our faith in the ultimate Healer, He will prepare the way; we will be supported, aided, and comforted. As Elder Jeffrey R. Holland said in his masterful address, "Cast Not Away Therefore Your Confidence":

> Along with the illuminating revelation that points us toward a righteous purpose . . . God will also provide the means and power to achieve that purpose. Trust in that eternal truth. If God has told you something is right, if something is indeed true for you, he will provide the way for you to accomplish it. . . . The Lord would tell Joseph again and again. . . . "Therefore, let not your hearts faint. . . : Mine angel shall go up before you. . . . and also my presence, and in time ye shall possess the goodly land. (Brigham Young University address, 2 March 1999; italics in original)

Elder Holland goes on to explain what the "goodly land" is: "Your promised land. Your new Jerusalem. Your own little acre flowing with milk and honey. Your future. Your dreams. Your destiny."

For those struggling with clinical depression or other illnesses or afflictions, the bright future, dreams, and promised land Elder Holland speaks of can seem far away. However, just as we have experienced the pain and heartache of clinical depression, we have become witnesses to the fact that healing from this form of mental illness can be a reality; and not only that, but that suffering in all its forms can be mitigated by the power of the Atonement (see Alma 7:11–13).

Through the light of the gospel, we come to understand that suffering is not meaningless: Through our pain, we fulfill one of the fundamental purposes of mortality—to become acquainted with our Savior and our Heavenly Father and to learn by faith that They are intimately involved in our lives, that They love us, and that They know us by name. "And this is life eternal, that they might know thee the only true God, and Jesus Christ, whom thou hast sent" (John 17:3).

Whatever price we pay for that knowledge pales in comparison to the blessings promised us: eternal life in the presence of He who is the source of all light, all truth, all hope, and all love.

And so we begin this book with our testimonies—we who thought we would never know joy in this life bear witness that with God, all things truly are possible.

—G.G., Gregory, and David Vandagriff

PART ONE
G.G.'S STORY

ONE

All manner of afflictions—Alma 62:50

Allow me to paint a word picture for you. You've wanted to go to the Italian countryside all your life, and now the moment you've dreamed of is here.

You are standing on a hill with tall grass and cornflowers waving around you. It is springtime, and the breeze is gentle with just a kiss of warmth. Above you the sky is as blue as something from an impressionist's paint box—so deep a blue that it verges on periwinkle. There are no clouds, but the sun is gentle, caressing you as it sits on your shoulders. The trees around the meadow are heavy with sweet-smelling, ivory-white pear blossoms. In the distance, you can see Florence—ancient and mellow, the muddy green Arno River running through it. You can just make out the cathedral, and you can vaguely hear the bells tolling their achingly deep tones. Your spouse is standing beside you. The sacrifice of this person, whose sole object is to please you, has made this whole experience possible. Out of nowhere, a string quartet begins to play Vivaldi.

You feel nothing. Your heart is dead. Everything might as well be ashes.

"Is it everything you dreamed?" your spouse asks, looking into your face with concerned hopefulness.

"Yes," you lie, overcome with guilt because your stone heart cannot even feel gratitude or love toward this person. In that moment, you feel like the most wretched, horrible person on earth. You have everything anyone could want, and yet you are miserable. You would even welcome death to stop the only thing you can feel—deep, yawning, black despair.

But you fear death because you know you will be damned by a God who must despise you for your inability to feel grateful for what you have and for your failure to exercise faith, hope, or charity.

* * *

This scene paints a picture of the hopelessness and despair felt by a person caught in the grips of a life-threatening illness—an illness that is as real as cancer. Depression.

When you have depression, the only thing that seems to exist inside you is a void so deep and so dark that you alternately fear for your life on the one hand, and wish for extinction on the other. You echo Nephi's anguished cry, "O wretched man that I am! Yea, my heart sorroweth because of my flesh; my soul grieveth because of mine iniquities. . . . And when I desire to rejoice, my heart groaneth because of my sins" (2 Nephi 4: 17–19).

Though you have not transgressed in any major way, you cry along with Alma, "O Jesus, thou Son of God, have mercy on me, who am in the gall of bitterness, and am encircled about by the everlasting chains of death" (Alma 36:18).

You tell yourself, "I am not worthy of a priesthood blessing, but if anything could cure me, surely it could." You seek many such blessings, but you feel nothing of the hope they offer. It seems the love of God simply cannot penetrate your breast. It is as though your heart were encased in a lead shield. When you have depression, your nervous system stops functioning properly, which means that all the nerve endings that should be communicating the visual and sensory details of the scene before you—as well as the love you should be feeling for your spouse, your children, and your Creator—are not doing their job. You cannot feel because, in a very literal sense, your brain is broken.

The only thing that sometimes helps disperse the darkness is sitting in the purest place on earth: the celestial room of the temple. Once in a great while, for a few moments, the anguish leaves. Although you are not happy, at least you are not tormented. But even if you go to the temple daily, you cannot live out your life in the celestial room.

The time comes that you can no longer leave your home; you are plagued by anxiety, which brings on panic attacks as you fight for each breath. Your body becomes numb from hyperventilation until you cannot even walk unassisted. You never know when or where another attack will strike. You might even be stricken when you're quietly sitting in church. And sometimes these attacks last for hours.

After many years, you give up on hoping for a miracle. You know vaguely, in some part of your being, that if there is any hope left, it resides in holding fast to the iron rod. You pray that when death finally comes, you will still be holding onto it.

Will there ever be an end to the suffering? You foresee only a gray, embattled future, where each day becomes a test of survival. You feel completely alone in your leaden shell. You are certain that no one and nothing can reach you.

Does such a description seem a bit extreme? Would a just God allow a person to exist in such a state? Part of the answer is found in understanding that depression is like any other illness. It is not a judgment but a condition of mortality. A broken brain is a physical condition—it has no more to do with personal righteousness than the ravaging physical effects of cancer. However, a key difference between depression and other illnesses is that the symptoms of depression are largely mental and emotional. A depressed person can rarely feel anything but blankness. When you are depressed, it is very unusual to be able to feel the Spirit—not because you have sinned, but because you can't feel *any* positive emotions: hope, joy, peace, happiness, charity, or love. For this reason, as Elder Alexander B. Morrison has counseled, a depressed person must be careful of the buffetings of the adversary. "Those who suffer from mental illness, who are burdened with pain, depression, and confusion must, I believe, be especially on their guard against the devil and his agents" ("Mental Illness and the Family," paper presented at the Brigham Young University Families Under Fire Conference, Provo, UT, October 4–5, 2004).

* * *

How do I know in such exquisite detail what it is like to live with this illness? I suffered from depression for twenty-five years. During the twenty-five years I suffered from depression, I raised a family. I wrote three books that were published. I held positions of responsibility in the Church. Twice, I was a bishop's wife. And yet each morning I woke up wishing that this would be the day I would be allowed to return to my Heavenly Father.

I first began to suffer with depression in college. After I had wrestled with the symptoms of hopelessness, despair, and fatigue for some time, I went to the student health center—which repeatedly diagnosed me as being pregnant! They refused to believe I wasn't until blood tests convinced them. Depression as an illness was not understood at that time.

After my second child was born, I found that I could not sleep. I went to my family doctor, who looked at me anxiously and began to explain what clinical depression was. I argued with him. I told him I was happy and not depressed. He explained that the chemicals in my nervous system were not working. He prescribed an antidepressant for me. That was in 1981. I continued to live my life, doing my best to cope. But by 1989, things had gotten worse; I was baffled by my symptoms, especially the way my body would simply shut down until I was completely disabled. At times I couldn't move or speak. A dear friend told me I needed to go to a psychiatrist. It was a three-hour drive. She went with me.

To my surprise, after giving me a lengthy test, the psychiatrist told me that I was 107 percent depressed and that I needed to be hospitalized for a month. From that point on, nothing was ever the same for me or my family. As I've looked deeper into my family history, I've discovered I'm part of a long line of those who've suffered with this disease. I've also learned that I'm the first person in my family, as far back as I can trace my genealogy, who has not been institutionalized for life because of this genetic disorder.

How did I endure? Most of the time, I told myself I was hanging on only because I knew that my suicide would scar my children and husband beyond anything I could imagine.

Now, looking back, I believe what got me through those blank, dead, heavy years was that I was enabled just enough by the power of the Atonement of Jesus Christ to keep going, to keep my eye on the distant goal that one day Jesus Himself would put His arms around me and say, "G.G., well done, thou good and faithful servant." I pictured Him holding my face in His hands and saying, "You are healed." I imagined eyes so deeply compassionate that they knew every pain I had endured, looking into mine with a love so intense that their very warmth would heal me completely.

I never thought it would happen in this life.

TWO

Wilt thou comfort my soul in Christ—Alma 31:31

While it's true that there are incredible medications that can help one's brain chemistry to function normally, as the years slipped by after my diagnosis with depression, none of them seemed to work for me. I was hospitalized for acute suicidality many times, had electro-convulsive therapy, and went through years and years of psychotherapy. As a result of electro-convulsive therapy in 2001, I lost large parts of my memory, including the ability to write (which had been my saving grace) and my ability to take photographs. I even forgot how I had gained seventy-five pounds and purchased an entire wardrobe of black clothes! As time went on, my children moved away from home, which increased my perceptions that life held no purpose for me. There was nothing left that the doctors hadn't tried. For three years, I woke up each morning facing blank panic. How was I going to get through the day?

In 2004, my life began to change dramatically when my husband was called to be the bishop of a BYU singles ward. Our stake president had a program: we were to intensely study the Atonement. Every prayer, talk, or lesson was to be related to the Atonement. At this point in my life, I only understood that the Atonement provided a means to be forgiven. I had no idea of the healing power it would bring to my life as I began to study it in earnest.

A major turning point for me came in the April 2004 general conference, when I heard a talk on the Atonement by Elder Bruce C. Hafen. I will never forget his words. They went straight to my heart:

We need grace both to overcome sinful weeds and to grow divine flowers. We can do neither one fully by ourselves. But grace is not cheap. It is very expensive, even very *dear*. How much does this grace cost? Is it enough simply to believe in Christ? The man who found the pearl of great price gave "all that he had" for it. If we desire "all that [the] Father hath," God asks *all that we have.* To qualify for such exquisite treasure, in whatever way is ours, we must give the way Christ gave—every drop He had: "How exquisite you know not, yea, how hard to bear you know not." Paul said, *"If so be that we suffer with him"* we are "joint-heirs with Christ." All of His heart, all of our hearts. . . . If we must give all that we have, then our giving only *almost* everything is not enough. If we *almost* keep the commandments, we *almost* receive the blessings. . . .

Some people want to keep one hand on the wall of the temple while touching the world's "unclean things" with the other hand. We must put both hands on the temple and hold on for dear life. One hand is not even *almost* enough. (Bruce C. Hafen, "The Atonement: All for All," *Ensign,* May 2004, 97–99; italics in original)

The idea of giving absolutely *everything* to, in turn, receive everything shouldn't have been new to me, but it was. During Elder Hafen's talk, one thought in particular impressed itself upon my mind. I had been holding on to my professed beliefs in the gospel with one hand, but with the other, I clung tightly to coping mechanisms and distractions in an attempt to keep the emptiness and the despair at bay. Until that time, in order to cope with my illness, I had been operating on a reward system—my way of filling the empty pain inside me. It worked like this: If I did everything I *had* to do in a day, I could reward myself by doing the only thing in the world I wanted to do—read. Now, I'm not saying there's anything wrong with reading. After all, you're reading this book. But I carried it to excess. I read at least a novel a day. And my reading material was not always uplifting. The only thing I demanded was a happy ending. Though I had a Stanford education, I was reading at a comic-book level. I consumed books like boxes of chocolates. The frothier, the better, as long as I could escape my pain for awhile.

During Elder Hafen's talk, I realized I'd literally been trying to rely on my reading to save my life. When I was reading, I wasn't thinking. And when I wasn't thinking, I wasn't depressed. It seemed to work . . . sometimes. But I began to realize that it was a form of addiction—and that I could not be holding on to the saving principles of the gospel and the Atonement with both hands if I was clinging so desperately to this distraction.

Elder Hafen was offering me a better solution. A truly lifesaving solution. If I would give up my cobbled-together substitute and allow the Savior's Atonement to fill the emptiness, I could begin to make some real progress in my life instead of just enduring.

I donated all my less-than-uplifting reading material to the library and started working at the temple two days a week. Working was very difficult and demanded all I had to give, but I knew the adversary couldn't reach me during those two days. I found strength in knowing that I was serving God and that I walked where the Savior walked. I also volunteered at the Missionary Training Center one day a week. I still read, as time permitted, but I changed my reading habits. On Sundays, I limited myself strictly to gospel reading.

The change in me was gradual at first. I realized I had a giant well of resentment and anger because I had this *dumb* illness that made it impossible for me to live a normal life. By this time in my life, I had become severely crippled by anxiety and could scarcely leave the house. Going to the temple and the MTC were tremendous acts of will. I was afraid of everything. But when I entered the temple or the MTC, the anxiety dropped from me like an unneeded cloak. The temple is a sacred place, and while we perform holy ordinances there, we do so by priesthood power. And thus we become sanctified by our service, little by little. The elderly women I worked with were angels. Learning of their often difficult lives and what they had endured and partaking of the sweet elixir of their self-sacrifice and indomitable faith was healing to my deadened spirit. I began to believe that it was possible to make it through the gauntlet of life. Watching the missionaries struggle with new experiences and an uncertain future gave me courage as well.

I asked to be assigned to the celestial room. I used this time to make promises to the Lord, to plead for mercy and grace, and to return and report each week. Things which had once seemed like insurmountable obstacles in my life began to seem more manageable. My concern for my son, Greg, who also struggled with depression—and who you will hear from later in this book—had been all-consuming. Gradually, over a period of a year, I began to see my prayers for my son answered. Week by week, things improved until he was ready to serve a mission. This was a true miracle.

As I saw the positive changes beginning to happen in my life, I began to rely on the Atonement with greater confidence and to let go of the other things I had used to replace the pain. I came to believe in the scripture in Alma 7:11–12 with all my heart.

> And he shall go forth, suffering pains and afflictions and temptations of every kind; and this that the word might be fulfilled which saith he will take upon him the pains and the sicknesses of his people.
>
> And he will take upon him death, that he may loose the bands of death which bind his people; and he will take upon him their infirmities, that his bowels may be filled with mercy, according to the flesh, that he may know according to the flesh how to succor his people according to their infirmities.

This scripture strengthened my faith that the Lord wouldn't condemn me for my weakness. It also gave me badly-needed instruction—I was to give the Savior the problems that were too difficult for me to bear. I knew, for example, that I would not be able to bear watching my son struggling, alone. I was fighting so hard to keep myself alive that I couldn't help him. I had to rely on the Lord to help me shoulder that burden. I remember kneeling by my bed, telling the Lord I was at the edge of my endurance and was ready to fall off. I pleaded with Him to take care of Greg. He did. It took longer than I expected, but Greg was taken care of, and he was blessed with healing when the time was right.

THE DIVINE VOID

As I began to hold on to the Atonement with both hands, I learned some important principles. One of the most important things I learned during this time was that in order to fully understand the Atonement, we must also understand the Fall. There are many hidden treasures to be gained from a prayerful study of Adam and Eve's story. Why do we hear their story each time we go to the temple? Why is their story told twice in the standard works? One day it came to me with stunning simplicity: their story is given to us as a prototype for our own lives. They were the first ones to experience what I have dubbed, "The Divine Void."

When Adam and Eve were cast out of the garden, they were left with an immense emptiness that nothing could fill—a space that had once been filled by direct discourse with and love of their Creator. Can you imagine what that must have been like? They had been deprived of the Light of the World, which had been with them since their creation. That great peace, that overwhelming comfort, that sure wisdom with answers to every question, was suddenly gone! The void the eternal presence left must have been immense.

Adam and Eve endeavored the rest of their lives to make their way back to where they had been, to regain that at-one-ment once again. Because they had experienced God's presence, they understood much better than we do that the only way we can fill the void is with divine help.

Because a veil is drawn across our minds when we are born, we each have a divine void in our lives. For the very fortunate, the emptiness is filled, to some extent, by a family who offers unconditional love, righteous role models, and instruction on how to receive forgiveness and salvation.

But most of the world is not so fortunate, and most are left with a dark well of emptiness they can't understand. They seek to fill it in many ways. Many good people succeed in filling it by loving and serving their fellow man—with sacrifice and selflessness. They find this gives them a sense of fulfillment that they can't experience in any other way. It is a paradox that the more we give, the more we are filled. As our Savior said, "Whosoever will lose his life for my sake shall find it" (Matthew 16:25). As Elder Holland said, speaking of the Savior in his general conference talk, "Broken Things to Mend":

"Trust me, learn of me, do what I do. Then, when you walk where *I* am going . . . we can talk about where *you* are going, and the problems you face and the troubles you have. If you will follow me, I will lead you out of darkness." . . . . He knows the way out and He knows the way up. . . . He knows the way because He *is* the way. (*Ensign,* May 2006, 69–71; italics in original)

But for those of us who do not understand this idea or have never been taught these principles (which includes most of the world), we seek to fill that divine void with other things, dulling our senses so we can't feel the emptiness. That was why I read compulsively—I used stories to replace the empty ache I felt. Other people use alcohol, drugs, sexual misconduct, extreme adrenaline producing activities, overindulgence in anything, and even their relationships with friends and spouses. Though going the latter route is proceeding in the right direction, even friends and family cannot completely fill the void. There is, after all, only one friend who will never fail us under any circumstances, and that is Jesus Christ.

The Atonement of Jesus Christ is the *only* thing that can fill that void. We are born with a longing for home, for Him. We are shown the way home in the Lord's house, where we are blessed with the ultimate ordinances in our journey. As we make and keep covenants and receive these ordinances in His house, we are made whole, and the at-one-ment that Adam and Eve sought can be obtained.

As we strive to become truly whole, we must seek the healing power of the Atonement to fill our wells with living water, and then give and give and give to those who have not so that they may see the model. They are then enabled, along with us, to follow the path shown by Adam and Eve, to find their way back to our loving Heavenly Father. This void is endemic to our existence. It may be the greatest of all our mortal trials, because it magnifies every other trial. If we are to avoid destructive, addictive, self-defeating behavior, we must learn to fill the void—to grasp with both hands the redemption offered by the Atonement of Jesus Christ.

THREE

An enabling power—Elder Bednar

I continued to make a concerted effort to access the power of the Atonement in my life. Each day brought new obstacles to overcome, and I knew I had much to learn. I was impressed by a comment that Elder Bednar made in speaking of the "enabling power of the Atonement." In discussing this power, he quotes the definition of "grace" in the Bible Dictionary:

> The main idea of the word is divine means of help or strength, given through the bounteous mercy and love of Jesus Christ. . . .
>
> It is likewise through the grace of the Lord that individuals, through faith in the atonement of Jesus Christ and repentance of their sins, receive strength and assistance to do good works that they otherwise would not be able to maintain if left to their own means. This grace is an enabling power that allows men and women to lay hold on eternal life and exaltation after they have expended their own best efforts." ("In the Strength of the Lord," *Ensign*, November 2004, 76–78)

I knew that if anyone had needed grace or enabling power, I did. Once confident as an economics and American politics college instructor, I was now terrified even to make a comment in Gospel Doctrine class. And I was the bishop's wife! The cheerful, brilliant BYU students expected me to speak at their firesides and activities at the drop of a hat—and yet there was no way they could comprehend my disability. What could I possibly say about the gospel that they didn't already know? It was at this time I learned that the Atonement does not simply fill a void in our lives—it is an active power that lifts, propels, and strengthens us. I began to rely on this enabling power to give me the confidence, strength, and ability I lacked. Soon I learned there was one thing I could always preach about with confidence: the Atonement! I did so at every opportunity.

A NEW CHALLENGE

I felt grateful for the deeper connection I felt to the Savior through the power of the Atonement. However, just as the pieces of the puzzle began to come together, new complications arose, and with them a greater need than ever for the enabling power of the Atonement.

Since 2001, I had been having increasingly severe panic attacks, the cause of which I didn't fully understand. In February of 2006, my condition worsened, and I became catatonic, unable to move or speak. My body was playing dead. I had been diagnosed with what's known as post-traumatic stress disorder, or PTSD, which has depression as one of its primary symptoms. The basis of PTSD is that a person may, for years, deny the trauma he or she has faced, plunging the reality deep into the subconscious in order to numb the pain. The problem is, one day the beleaguered nervous system simply can't handle the unresolved trauma anymore. This is what had begun happening to me in 2001. Painful memories and feelings I had kept buried for years had began to surface—and it was too much for my fragile body.

My therapist identified the trigger of my PTSD as anger. Anger shown by others, as well as anger unexpressed inside me. The abuse I had suffered many years previously was cankering my soul. I thought I had forgiven the abusers, but the panic attacks were evidence that I had not healed from the abuse. Although my body was being treated with high doses of antianxiety medicine, I knew that a full healing would require my spirit to be treated as well.

For several years, my symptoms worsened. I moved into the next phase of the disorder, in which I cried uncontrollably for no apparent reason. Then the flashbacks began, and I experienced full-blown PTSD. It was the closest thing to Gethsemane I ever hope to experience. All the pain of the traumatic incidents I had experienced over a course of more than two decades visited me at once and nearly crushed me. I had denied the pain in the past, but now I was feeling it. Every bit of it. At times, the only way out of the pain seemed to be suicide. It took hours of talking to trusted listeners to release the pain from my heart. I turned very bitter because I didn't understand the next step, which I knew only the Atonement could help me with. I knew I had to fully forgive my abusers in order to have the pain taken away—but I didn't know how.

It was the book *The Peacegiver* by James Ferrell (Deseret Book, 2004) that finally helped me understand how to take the next step toward healing. Using 1 Samuel 25, Brother Ferrell describes a seldom-told story from the Bible that is actually a type of the Atonement. As I heard this story for the first time, I began to understand that until we fully forgive others, we cannot completely understand or access the Atonement ourselves.

The account goes like this. David is living in the wilderness as an outlaw with a band of men. He is on the run from Saul, who seeks his life. In order to feed themselves, David and his men offer to protect the sheep and the shepherds belonging to a wealthy man named Nabal. When the season is over and the sheep are being shorn, David and his men await their payment. However, instead of paying David and his men with the desired provisions, Nabal says, "Who is David? and who is the son of Jesse? there be many servants now a days that break away every man from his master. Shall I then take my bread, and my water, and my flesh that I have killed for my shearers, and give it unto men, whom I know not whence they be?" (1 Samuel 25:10–11).

Upon hearing this deeply insulting and ungrateful reply, David, the rightful king of Israel, "gird[s] on every man his sword" (v. 13). He and four hundred of his men determine to march on Nabal and kill the men in his household in revenge. But one of Nabal's servants, who knows of the justice of David's claim, goes to Nabal's wife, Abigail, and discloses the threat.

The account continues. "Then Abigail made haste, and took two hundred loaves, and two bottles of wine, and five sheep ready dressed, and five measures of parched corn, and an hundred clusters of raisins, and two hundred cakes of figs, and laid them on asses" (v. 18). Without telling her husband, she rides down to intercept David and his men.

The next part of the account arrested my soul. "And when Abigail saw David, she hasted, and lighted off the ass . . . and bowed herself to the ground, [a]nd fell at his feet, and said, Upon me, my lord, upon me let this iniquity be: and let thine handmaid, I pray thee, speak in thine audience, and hear the words of thine handmaid" (vv. 23–24). Abigail then tells David that she knows her husband is evil, but she knows that David is a just man who is bound to be the king of Israel. She begs him to take her reparation instead of slaying Nabal and becoming a murderer: "That this shall be no grief unto thee, nor offence of heart unto my lord, either that thou hast shed blood cause-less, or that my lord hath avenged himself: but when the Lord shall have dealt well with my lord, then remember thine handmaid" (v. 31).

In his book, Brother Ferrell explains that Abigail is a type of Christ and that she is offering herself in the stead of her husband to appease David's wrath and save him from committing murder. This story struck me profoundly. Could I too look upon the Savior as the mediator between me and my abusers? Would He also offer recom-pense for my pain and beg me on His behalf to stay my bitterness and my unforgiving heart? Could I forgive my abusers for His sake and allow Him to make His own judgment, thus not cankering my soul with bitterness and pain? I finally understood that not only could Christ's Atonement enable me to hold on, it could enable me to let go of pain and bitterness. And after all that I could do, He would step in as mediator to settle the scales of justice and mercy.

I began to see my abusers as wounded sheep, carried one by one on the shoulders of my Shepherd. I pictured the Savior looking into my eyes with a desperate plea, asking me to let go of my bitterness and to forgive each wounded one, who also had a claim on His love. I plainly felt His love for me, and I knew that in order for mercy to intervene on my behalf, I had to leave the wounded sheep to Him and trust in His wisdom, justice, and power to heal.

It took a major change of heart, for the world does not expect victims of abuse to forgive in this way, but I slowly felt my pain and bitterness begin to ebb away. How could I continue to despise my abusers when every time I thought of those people, I saw only wounded lambs and visualized Jesus Christ offering Himself in their place? A burden I had not even known I was carrying was lifted from my soul, and I was finally able to close the door on that chapter of my life. This paradigm shift in my understanding of forgiveness allowed me to trust the Savior as I never had before.

"WITH ALL THY HEART"

Changing one's heart through the Atonement can seem like an awesome task; however, just like any other facet of the gospel, we are not expected to change in one giant step. We move forward little by little. What the Lord does require us to give all at once is our hearts—our whole hearts. The Lord explained it very simply in His sermon at the temple recorded in 3 Nephi. The Savior told those present that He had fulfilled the law of Moses, and that now the sacrifice required of His listeners was not a "blood sacrifice," but something much harder. He wanted from them their very hearts. He said, "I have given you the law and the commandments of my Father, that ye shall believe in me, and that ye shall repent of your sins, and come unto me *with a broken heart and a contrite spirit*" (3 Nephi 12:19; emphasis added).

His followers were no longer required to look forward to His coming by making sacrifices in His similitude; instead, they were asked to literally become His. And how do we become His? The Lord is specific about this, as recorded in Matthew 22:37: "Thou shalt love the Lord thy God with all thy heart, and with all thy soul, and with all thy mind." *All. All* is the operative word. But how is that possible? This brings us back to Elder Hafen's talk on the Atonement:

> We must willingly give everything, because God Himself can't make us grow against our will and without our full participation. Yet even when we utterly spend ourselves, we lack the power to create the perfection only God can complete. Our *all* by itself is still only *almost* enough— until it is finished by the *all* of Him who is the "finisher of our faith." At that point, our imperfect but conse- crated *almost* is enough. ("The Atonement: All for All," 97–99; italics in original)

As Elder Hafen confirms, our first step in becoming His is conse- cration—giving all that we have and all that we are. But even though our best efforts are imperfect, they will still be consecrated to Him. On days when I could only give five percent—because five percent was my all—Christ made up the remaining ninety-five percent. As we strive to keep all aspects of our lives in tune with His will, our all will be enough because of the merits of Jesus Christ. We must be willing to get down on our knees, give up our fears, our sins, our "little cottage in Babylon," and "becometh as a child, submissive, meek, humble, patient, full of love, willing to submit to all things which the Lord seeth fit to inflict upon [us], even as a child doth submit to his father" (Mosiah 3:19).

This part of the Atonement—the relationship between us and the Lord— can be referred to as the vertical aspect of the Atonement. We must trust Him with childlike confidence, putting our very souls in His hands. We must trust that He is who He says He is, and that He knows the way. The vertical aspect of the Atonement implies a direct link between us and our Savior, and it requires that we rely on Him, placing our souls in His care.

People who have suffered from PTSD often struggle immensely with this. I was no exception; although I could forgive and was trying to do my part, I found it very difficult to *trust* in anyone, especially someone I couldn't even see. Because my trust had been repeatedly violated throughout my life, I had no experience with trusting unconditionally. I didn't think I could have the simple faith of a child. Being a child had been an incredibly frightening experience for me. Thus, I didn't want to give up my sense of control. *But I didn't understand that in many ways, I really had no control.* Despite all I had come to understand and the progress I had made, I was still holding back.

Within my limitations, I was still growing spiritually, and I felt grateful for what I had learned about the Atonement. It spurred me to make many changes. But there was still a lot to learn and much healing to take place. The void still yawned within me as I struggled to learn how to trust the Lord as He offered His hand to me.

With the worst of my PTSD behind me, I hoped that at last the time had come for me to climb steadily upward. However, just as I thought perhaps the storm was passing, events beyond my control exposed my worst fears and put my fledgling faith and trust to the test. External events—a death in the family, as well as a personal economic crisis— tipped me off my precarious ledge, and I went into the worst depression of my life.

FOUR

Trust in the Lord with all thine heart and lean not unto thine own understanding—Proverbs 3:5

Shortly before April 2006 general conference, I was obliged to give up working in the temple because, due to the increasingly difficult circumstances in my personal life, my panic attacks had grown so severe I couldn't function. Since the temple was my one source of refuge, I felt hopeless and bitter. My life was utterly dark. I sometimes thought of a devotional given by President Hugh B. Brown about the night before he was called to be an assistant to the Quorum of the Twelve Apostles. He said, "All night I wrestled with the evil spirit. I was possessed with the spirit of wishing that I could be rubbed out of existence. I had no thought of suicide, but wished the Lord would provide a way for me to cease to be. The room was full of darkness and an evil spirit prevailed, so real that I was almost consumed by it" (Edwin Brown Firmage, "Elder Hugh B. Brown, 1883–1975: In Memoriam," *Ensign,* January, 1976, 86–91). I felt he was describing perfectly the depths of my depression. Many days and nights I had struggled in just that way, thinking, "How can I end it if I don't end my life?"

We had conference tickets that year, and I was fortunate enough to hear Elder Holland's talk, "Broken Things to Mend," to which I have previously referred. I sat in wonder as he described my state of mind:

> I speak to those who are facing personal trials . . . those who endure conflicts fought in the lonely foxholes of the heart, those trying to hold back floodwaters of despair

that sometimes wash over us like a tsunami of the soul. I
wish to speak particularly to you who feel your lives are
broken, seemingly beyond repair. . . .

The surest and sweetest remedy that I know. . . . is
found in the clarion call the Savior of the world himself
gave. . . . "Come unto me, all ye that labour and are
heavy laden, and I will give you rest. Take my yoke
upon you, and learn of me; for I am meek and lowly in
heart: and ye shall find rest unto your souls." (*Ensign*,
May 2006, 69–71)

Oh! How I longed for that rest! My husband recorded Elder Holland's
talk for me, and I listened to it, sometimes several times daily as I endeavored to fight through my panic attacks. I visualized Peter walking toward
the Lord on the water, full of faith, and then, like me, doubting and falling
into the water. Drowning. But the Savior's arms were still stretched out to
him. He was rescued in spite of his doubts. I lay in bed, crying, wishing
the Savior would come for me.

Faith of any kind had always been hard for me, because in my
depressed state, I was without hope. This condition was endemic to
my illness. The cognitive symptoms of depression are defined as "excessive self-criticism; negativity and pessimism; excessive anxiety, guilt, and
anger; helplessness; low self-esteem; difficulty recognizing and believing
positives; brooding over the past; and *hopelessness*" (Mary L. Billingsley
and Thad H. Billingsley, *Depression: The Way Out*, [Shawnee Mission,
Kansas: The Benessere Center, 1987], 2; emphasis added).

But, as Elder Holland suggested in his address, I studied Alma 32 for
perhaps the thousandth time. I had the desire and I gave, as he counseled,
"a *small place* for the promises of God to find a home" (*Ensign*, May
2006, 69–71; italics in original). In my despair, I spent literally hours on
my knees petitioning the Lord for faith, for hope, for my survival, for
some kind of deliverance. My hold on life was precarious at best. I was as
thin as a pencil, shook like a leaf, and was thrown into a panic attack by
something as simple as a shower.

Just as I struggled with faith, I struggled with trust. I didn't know if
I could offer everything or leave the outcome in someone else's hands.

That would mean putting everything on the altar—including my husband, the one stable thing in my life. I had reached the point where I felt I could offer all my worldly possessions— that had not been an easy thing because of the insecurity I had faced during a period in our life when we were without income. I believed that the Lord had helped our family then and would help us now. But what if I were asked to give up the one thing I didn't think I could live without? How could I go on without my husband? I prayed and prayed for the ability to trust in the Savior. I knew I could not solve this on my own; I needed to give up my need to feel in control.

Then it dawned on me. This wasn't a matter of control. It was a matter of fear. I had no real control to begin with. I finally said, "Take everything. Do with it what You will. You can do a much better job with my life than I can. Whatever it takes, I want to belong to the Savior. I want that relationship to be paramount—to come before anything else. *I place myself completely on the altar.* I promise I will trust You no matter what happens; I trust You not to try me beyond that which I can bear."

I made myself totally vulnerable—a very frightening prospect for me. And I let go.

THE MIRACLE

Although I was very ill, I endeavored to reach out to others and live as closely to the Lord as possible. One day, as I was visiting teaching a new sister with a new companion, I had a panic attack. Neither of the sisters knew about my illness. With my husband serving as a campus bishop, I felt cut off from the members of my home ward, aside from visiting teaching. As I apologetically explained to them the nature of my illness, both sisters became very concerned. They suggested a Relief Society fast. I begged them not to do this. My depression was a twenty-five-year-old impossible affliction. There were too many other sisters who had far more serious problems. Two of them were dying. Nevertheless, unknown to me, my visiting teaching companion called several sisters and organized a fast for me. I didn't even know most of them.

At the time I also had a close friend whom I walked with on some mornings. She knew a lot about mental illness and had watched my recent decline with growing alarm. I had lost so much weight I was skeletal. I trembled constantly. I was afraid every minute of every day. I was angry that my one healing balm—temple service—had been denied me. I was bound by a blackness so profound I had great difficulty perceiving any light. She told me, "G.G., you are very sick. I've watched you. You need to go to the doctor. There must be something they can do for you." I told her that, on the contrary, my psychiatrist had told me there was nothing he could do for me. Every drug had been tried. Every treatment had been experimented with. I was on my own. As my therapist had told me, this was the way my body was wired. But my friend persisted, begging me to give it one more try.

I agreed, but I felt little hope. I knew my diagnosis, and I knew that the odds stacked against me weren't good. Because my depression was genetic, my nervous system did not make the proper combination of the three chemicals necessary for my nerve endings to transmit impulses from one to the other. When I said my brain was broken, it was the literal truth. My brain couldn't function properly, because there was no way for it to transfer impulses to my nervous system properly (see *Depression: The Way Out,* for a more detailed explanation of depression). I had tried many different types of medication, but none had helped. (Modern antidepressant treatment is in many ways guesswork, as each psychiatrist must experiment until they find the appropriate combination and dosage of chemicals an individual needs in order to function.) My case was one of the five percent considered untreatable, because no existing medications had worked for me.

Therefore, I was not expecting much when I made an appointment with my family doctor, a personal friend in my ward. My psychiatrist had given up on me, and I decided that I would see if my family doctor might at least be able to give me something to alleviate my anxiety. I wasn't able to get in to see him until the following week. I didn't know it then, but the day I saw the doctor was the day my friends were fasting for me.

When the doctor entered my cubicle, before I could say a word, he asked me what medications my psychiatrist had prescribed for my depression and anxiety. I told him. He said, "Let's see if we can do better than that. I found out about some new medications yesterday. I have some samples, and I'd like you to try them." He gave me two medications, both new.

Without much enthusiasm, I took both medications that night. I had been down this road so many times before, only to fail again and again.

Besides, antidepressants typically took weeks to work. I had very little hope, but I nonetheless remembered my commitment to the Lord and exercised a particle of faith, as Elder Holland had suggested.

The next morning, when I opened my eyes, *the blackness was gone.* Beautiful light streamed through my bedroom window, and a feeling of deep spiritual well-being filled my soul. The fear was gone. The years of blackness were gone. I was anxious to get up and begin this new day. I couldn't believe the way I felt. As I sat up, the world whirled around me, and I lay back down.

Side effects. Was I going to be able to tolerate these new medications? At that moment, I decided I didn't care if I had to live as a dizzy invalid, as long as I could be emotionally and mentally healthy. I had never felt this kind of peace in my life. I called my doctor and he assured me that, in time, the side effects would go away. Over the next three weeks, I gradually began to feel better physically. Emotionally, I improved daily. At first I was very tentative about the changes taking place. But within the first month, I felt my true personality emerging. Except for my husband, those around me had never known the real G.G. It was a major adjustment for them. They couldn't believe that this vibrant, happy woman was really me! My confidence grew, and I began to undertake projects and take advantage of opportunities. I was filled with a love for the Lord and my fellow man I'd never felt in my life. I had greater self-confidence. This was all new for me. As my true personality emerged during that first month, I was like a starving person who was eating for the first time in years. Everything tasted wonderful. I was euphoric.

I spent more time on my knees than I ever had, this time in tearful gratitude for the answer to twenty-five years of prayer. At last, the missing chemicals had been delivered to my brain, allowing the synapses of my nervous system to function as they should.

When I went back to my therapist, he said, "Your family doctor was clearly inspired. If you had gone to a psychiatrist with the symptoms you presented, he wouldn't have put you on those drugs. I really don't understand how they're working."

I knew without a doubt that I owed everything that had happened to my Savior and to those who fasted for me. I had placed my trust in Him, and He had not let me fall. I felt like a wind-up toy that had been fully wound, set in the right direction, and released!

It's been a year now, and the crippling fear I felt for so long has not returned. I can pray with a faith I had not previously been able to experience. I can actually *feel* the arms of my Savior's love. I know my Master, and I know He knows me. He has always known and loved me, but because of the mortal body I inherited, I simply could not feel it. Because of the grace and power of the Atonement of Jesus Christ, I have experienced a mighty change of heart, a miracle I never expected in mortality.

Lest anyone wonder exactly what the combination of drugs my doctor prescribed was, let me say it was a unique combination that could only have been hit upon by inspiration. And although the prescription truly was miraculous, there have still been many bumps in the road. I must still manage my illness and carefully monitor my health. One of the drugs has a side effect of weight gain. After gaining thirty-five pounds in six months, I went to my doctor and suggested we replace it with a different drug that had the same function. He had no qualms with this and immediately prescribed another medication for me. Little by little, I spiraled into a mania that went completely out of control. This lasted for three weeks, during which time I hardly slept. Finally, I crashed. I slept for days. It was only then that I linked the incidence of my mania with my switching medications. I began taking the original medication once more, and my mental equilibrium slowly returned. But it took weeks to get over the exhaustion and fear brought about from tampering with the inspired combination of chemicals.

I did not wholly learn my lesson from this experience, nor did my doctor, who was not experienced in treating complex mental illness. About two months after this I went to him again, complaining of fatigue. I was still sleeping around the clock. He looked at my medications and said, "I don't know why I ever put you on this medication. It doesn't make sense. Let's take you off of it. It causes fatigue."

Although a little wary, I nevertheless went off the one medication he was questioning. Within a week, I was in the pit of despair. I prayed fervently to know what to do. Immediately I felt an impression to return to the full dose of the discontinued medicine. (I had only been taking a half dose because of my fear of weight gain.) When I followed this impression, not only did my depression immediately disappear, but so did my fatigue.

It became even clearer to me at that time that the particular combination of medicines I was taking had been directly inspired by the Lord. I don't have the answers as to why this medication works the way it does for me. In reading about this particular medicine in pharmacological literature, I have not found a satisfactory explanation. It is simply the right chemical, in combination with my antidepressant, to enable my brain chemistry to work as it should.

If you have had trouble finding the right medication, my advice is to never give up. You will be guided, according to the Lord's timing, and you will be sustained in your trials. I was at the end of my rope; it seemed useless to try one more medication—especially one that was new. I had to learn to live with side effects I would have previously thought intolerable; however, even those eventually went away. (Except for the weight gain. But I would rather be plump than suicidal.) Don't give up.

LESSON LEARNED

As Elder Holland promised in his talk, "Christ's yoke is easy and His burden truly is light" ("Broken Things to Mend," 69). The time for me to be healed physically was finally right. All the pieces were in place. I was trying the best I could. My friends had exercised their faith by fasting in my behalf. My doctor, who was not specialized in treating mental illness, was given samples of the new medications the day before he saw me. My life was changed forever.

I understand that my healing began long before my doctor prescribed that combination of medications to heal my physical body. Although I am profoundly grateful for the miracle of modern medicine, I am most grateful for the miracle of the Atonement of Jesus Christ and my relationship with Him, which is at the base of any healing we undergo. Through the Atonement, I experienced healing little by little as I learned to forgive, trust, and endure to the end. Although I did not always understand the whys at the time, I look back now and see that I was never out of reach of His loving, guiding hands.

Now I can press forward with that heretofore elusive "perfect brightness of hope" (2 Nephi 31:20), to tackle new challenges as I hold fast to my faith in Jesus Christ, which has been forged in the fire of my extremities.

A friend who has known me these twenty-five years recently asked me if I'm bitter that the healing has taken so long. I reflected and confided, "No. It's kind of like the handcart pioneers. It took tremendous hardship for them to become acquainted with the Savior and the reality of the Atonement. The price I paid to know Him was almost half my life; but after all, that's what I came to earth for. To know God and His Only Begotten Son. Nothing else really matters."

Everyone experiences different trials here on earth. We all must pay a unique price as we learn to trust our Savior and put our lives completely into His watchful care. I tell you my story as a testimony of what the power of the Atonement has done—and continues to do—for me. I teach it to my children, I teach it to my friends, and I teach it to strangers through books and magazine articles.

I know that a cure is not always the outcome; however, even if the outcome is death, if you have an understanding of the vertical aspect of the Atonement in your life—a relationship with and faith in your relationship to the Lord—you have gained the most important thing you need from this earthly existence. It is helpful to remember Alma's people, who were in bondage to the Lamanites. They had this type of vertical relationship with the Savior, and He lightened their burdens so they could not feel them upon their backs until the day of their deliverance (see Mosiah 24).

Once you put everything you have to offer on the altar, you have paid your price to come to know God. You are truly His. And that is what our mortal life is all about. Not achieving, not accumulating, but *becoming*.

Elaine Shaw Sorensen, who spoke at the BYU Women's Conference in 1993, summarizes this principle well:

> Grace transcends mortal rules of justice. Life is not a mechanical scale of effort or suffering on one side balanced by the appropriate reward on the other. Life is a process of growth, where growth itself becomes the reward. I tired long ago of hearing promises of some future mortal reward equal to my suffering, as when well-meaning friends foresee financial security or loving companionship in a future whose happiness will

outweigh the sadness of my past. The deceiving logic of such an idea implies that when life goes on, droning with problems, with no glory in sight, I am not yet worthy or perhaps have not yet suffered enough. That is unsettling, when all around, those apparently less righteous or less tried seem to be reaping the glorious gifts of this earth.

The fact is that trials are neither distributed equally nor sorted according to a subsequent and matching earthly or heavenly treasure. Problems are neither price nor penance for credit toward some misconceived idea of payment. Instead, *life itself, even eternal life, with growth, hope, and peace promised by the Savior's atonement, becomes its own reward, offering divine gifts of the Spirit. The proving question is not What will I gain or achieve? but Who will I become?* ("Evening Balm and Morning Manna: Daily Gifts of Healing Grace," in Elaine Shaw Sorensen, *Women in the Covenant of Grace: Talks Selected from the 1993 Women's Conference;* [Salt Lake City: Deseret Book, 1994], 268; emphasis added)

Since I have been given back my life, I have developed a new relationship with the Lord where I truly understand what He wants me to do each day. I try to dedicate each day to Him and to prioritize according to that which is most important spiritually, not temporally. In this way, I have given my life over to Him to do with it what He will. And amazing things have happened in my life. At age fifty-nine, I have at last embarked on the mission the Lord charged me with in my patriarchal blessing. I have been given incredible opportunities; for example, I have grown in my ability to write and to speak publicly, when for the past twelve years, I had been able to do neither. Now, the Lord provides me almost daily with opportunities to do both. I will publish three books this year. I have been called to bear witness of my recovery in many places at many times. I have a whole new circle of friends I am working with, helping them to experience the miracle of the Atonement in their lives. I will live the remainder of my life as a witness to the reality of the Atonement and the reality that the only way to truly change the world is one heart at a time.

PART TWO
GREGORY'S STORY

FIVE

*And all these things shall give thee experience—*D&C 122:7

Somewhere between age twelve and thirteen, I was diagnosed with clinical depression. I was less than thrilled.

Depression, in my mind, was nothing more than the illusion of a feeble, frenzied mind—a quasi-real sickness conjured up to ease the pain of those with weak wills. I was admitted to a mental hospital shortly after my initial diagnosis with clinical depression; however, the brief time I spent in that place only served to cement my denial as I compared my so-called illness to disorders like schizophrenia, severe bipolar depression, and the like. When all was said and done, I reluctantly (and faithlessly) took my prescribed antidepressants only to placate my parents.

It was around this time that my personality began to change. My moods began to darken as I gradually became more pessimistic, cynical, bitter, and jaded about life and other people. Eventually, my cynicism graduated to total apathy. I began to withdraw into myself, emotionally and physically. I soon found myself preferring the fantastic realms of science fiction and fantasy movies, books, and video games—these were my only escape from the dark, foreboding feelings of uneasiness, anxiety, and fear I harbored within.

During my high school years, I became a social outcast. I never quite seemed to feel at home with any group; I didn't even feel like I fit in with my fellow science fiction and fantasy fans. I knew, somewhere inside of me, that I could do so much more with my life than I was choosing to do. This uncomfortable feeling of loneliness eventually crept deeper and deeper into my crowded emotional state.

By the time college came around, I had begun to manifest my emotions through my appearance. Like some sort of delayed onset of teen angst, I sought attention through rebellion and audaciously bold and confrontational behavior. I tried to hide my insecurities from the world beneath black clothing and intimidating behavior. I vowed I would rather be feared than forgotten, and my perception of the world grew darker in spite of the obvious concern displayed by those who cared most for me. Eventually, I turned my back on my friends as well as my God, falling into inactivity in the Church. But even this wasn't enough for me—misery loves company. And so I began to actively discourage my friends from attending church or serving missions.

At the time, this seemed like the only thing to do. My poor choices to embrace the natural man invariably led to a downward spiral in my social, spiritual, academic, and physical health. My life was coming apart at the seams, and I completely broke down. I dropped out of college and returned home, humiliated by my inability to cope with "the real world," yet prideful nevertheless. My heart remained hardened, my outlook bleak. My emotional state became even more unstable as I wrestled with the sudden loss of a relationship with a certain young lady. I felt utterly rejected, broken, and embarrassed. What had become of me?

It was in April 2004 that a turning point occurred. My initial game plan was to simply accept my parents' invitation to watch general conference out of respect for the sacrifice they were making in housing and feeding me at the time. After all, what did I have to lose? Only a couple of hours that would have otherwise been spent bemoaning my seemingly pointless existence.

As I watched the Saturday afternoon session of conference to appease my parents, a strange thing happened. I felt something peculiar inside me, a feeling of peace, comfort, and quiet joy. For the first time in my memory, I felt driven to pray. I did not pray out of tradition. I did not pray because it was the thing to do or because of family pressure. That night I knelt down and prayed because I had a lot in my heart, including questions that needed answers. One of those questions was whether or not God listened to prayers.

He does. He heard my prayer that night. I didn't experience a huge transformation where the next morning I arose with a different outlook on life, magically healed of my depression, and radiating joy in every direction. However, I did awake the next morning with the desire to have such a transformation take place. And I knew I needed to serve a mission.

I met with my bishop immediately and began the long, arduous journey back into full activity. Over the course of the next year, I prepared myself to serve the Lord. It was not an easy thing, but after that year, I was declared fit for missionary service by a number of mental health professionals and ecclesiastical leaders.

Halfway through my mission, I was blessed to be able to switch the medications I was taking; this enabled me to experience a life-changing awakening of my emotional and spiritual faculties on a massive scope. I was able to feel the redeeming power of the Atonement more strongly than ever before, and the enabling power of the Atonement blessed me with a strength and power I had not previously been able to fathom. For the first time in my life, I felt alive and capable of sustaining that feeling indefinitely. I felt like I actually had a choice about my perspective, my attitude, and my mood.

Did my life suddenly become easier? No. I've learned that life has plenty of challenges for everyone at any level of mental health. However, I no longer felt hopelessly overwhelmed by my challenges. I felt like I had a fighting chance against Satan and his minions of despair for the first time I could remember. I felt like I could make an offensive stand against the adversary instead of constantly fighting on the defensive.

The chapters that follow contain the lessons my mission experiences taught me about the nature of depression—and how to conquer it.

SIX

Ye will always abound in good works—Alma 7:24

I believe many people suffering from clinical depression would agree that one of the most frustrating and crucial battles associated with this illness is getting motivated to work, to do something, to do *anything*. And the ability to act, to do something, is crucial because our self-worth is, in large measure, derived from our actions and from the impact that we have on the world. Furthermore, when we are idle, we have a tendency to dwell on ourselves and our problems. The most frustrating part of this is that we can easily become caught in a vicious cycle of self-pity and apathy, which leads to inaction and subsequently a continual worsening of our mental and emotional state.

This cycle can often lead to our receiving labels such as "lazy" or "inconsistent" from those around us. I have found that over time, these labels tend to stick in our minds, and we start to actually believe them. This eventually leads us to focus on the effects of the cycle and not the cause. We try to be less "lazy" and more consistent, and when we constantly meet with failure because of an underlying lack of strong motivation, it in turn leads to more frustration, more anger, and more apathy and hopelessness.

The adversary would have us believe that we are helpless and that there is no way out of the darkness. And he often succeeds. These cycles are spiritually damning, as they prevent us from growing and overcoming our weaknesses. Instead of facing our obstacles, we turn and flee from them. As we do so, we grow weaker, while our perceived obstacles grow ever stronger.

Is there a way out? Is there hope?

Perhaps one of the most critical lessons I learned in the mission field was that it is indeed possible to break out of these cycles. It is not easy, but if we have faith, and if we are willing to humble ourselves, all things are possible.

The key is to find, nurture, and follow an infallible source of motivation higher than ourselves. People use many motivators, each of which varies in quality and value. However, the majority of these motivators is fallible and can lead to a vicious relapse.

When serving in the mission field, I learned a critical lesson about the importance of this principle. I often found myself witness to a peculiar phenomenon. Let's take two fictitious elders, Elder Brown and Elder Smith. Both are phenomenal missionaries from the get-go. They launch into their missions like celestial fireballs, preaching the gospel and crying repentance with boldness, diligence, and obedience. They touch the hearts of all they come in contact with, and they are honest, sincere, and hardworking. They seem unstoppable.

Eighteen months into their missions, though, something happens. Let's say that each of these fine young men gets an unexpected wedding invitation from his girlfriend. The result? Elder Smith begins to slide into disobedience, idleness, and apathy. Elder Brown continues to press forward and finishes his mission with honor. Elder Smith is sent home dishonorably after twenty-one months.

The "Dear John" phenomenon can teach us a lot about the importance of having a proper and solid motivation. In the above example, both elders were strongly motivated to be their very best; the only difference was their motivations. Elder Smith was motivated to be a rock-solid, returned missionary husband to his high school sweetheart; his goal was to impress her and to fulfill her expectations of him. Elder Brown, on the other hand, was motivated by a desire to serve the Lord Jesus Christ; he recognized that no matter what happened, this source of motivation would never fail him.

As a result of their different sources of motivation, both elders responded differently to the same event. The wedding invitation destroyed Elder Smith's motivation for serving a mission. He had done all this work for eighteen months for someone he couldn't really count on, someone who had left him high and dry. Elder Brown, however, knew that the eighteen months he had put in so far weren't for the girl back home, but for the Lord, and so he continued to press on, enduring to the end.

This example can be expanded and applied to any circumstances. I went through this process several times on my mission: my fallible motivators included things such as impressing the mission president, being an example to my friends back home, being an example to other missionaries, and so forth.

While on my mission, I constantly fell back into my vicious cycles of depression. It wasn't until serving under my third mission president that I finally recognized the problem—my motivations were fallible. It was then I realized that the motivator I should have been using all along was right there on my nametag—Jesus Christ.

When I determined to make the Savior my motivation, my mission took off, and my depression faded into the background. Unlike a relationship with another person, a relationship with the Savior is completely unconditional, constant, and infallible. This is the beauty of the Atonement. No matter how many times we fail, the Savior will forgive us and help us get back on our feet.

This is also why prayer and scripture study are so crucial if we are to be successful in surviving depression and the vicious cycles it creates. Constant communication strengthens our relationship with the Savior and helps us to increase our desire to serve Him with all of our heart, might, mind, and strength.

Additionally, if we stop praying or studying the scriptures, we become like the aforementioned elder who stopped writing his girlfriend and therefore stopped receiving mail from her. We lose our desire to work because we are neglecting the very relationship that motivated us to succeed in the first place.

SEVEN

A perfect brightness of hope—2 Nephi 31:20

There are very few things in life that can compare with the misery associated with the emotion of hopelessness. For me, at least, one of the most major manifestations of my clinical depression was a significant lack of hope regarding almost everything. This cloud of hopelessness descended upon me gradually, and by the time I was in junior high, I'd lost hope that I would ever achieve success in any aspect of my life. This led to the formation of a negative, cynical, darkly humorous, and sarcastic attitude.

It is frustrating to look back and realize that after only a short period of time, I came to sincerely believe that my bleak and biting attitude was just part of my "natural" personality, part of the real me. My perception of my own personality had been skewed by my hopelessness. And that hopelessness led me to believe that I couldn't do anything to change that personality. Why would I want to, anyway? I had developed the personality to protect my insecurities in the first place. It's always easier to magnify and mock the failures of others than to attempt to succeed yourself.

This was my attitude throughout high school and my freshman year in college. However, the problem with having a negative personality is that on the inside, you're always so afraid of failure that you never dare to do great things. This fear spills over into your relationships, and you tend to drain those around you of their hope. Those who are doing great things will, in turn, generally choose not to be around you as they become aware of the draining effect of your cynicism.

As I persisted in embracing hopeless mediocrity in my lifestyle, friendships, and future, I discovered that things did not ever improve. If anything, they worsened as I progressively settled for less and did less and less with my life until all hope was burned out. When I eventually reached this point, it was devastating. I withdrew from BYU and returned home seeking help and stability. The temporary boosts of hope I felt from my parents and siblings never seemed to last. It felt like I was pouring my hope into an emotional bucket, but instead of staying in there like it should, it would quickly drain through a hole in the bottom of the bucket, leaving it as empty as it began.

I would learn on my mission, however, that there are ways to keep the bucket filled almost constantly—allowing a person to have hope, which leads to faith, which leads to action, which eventually can lead to success. It is not easy, but it is possible.

I first recognized this principle when I saw that although some missionaries seemed to be able to maintain their work ethic with lazy scripture study and rote prayers, I was definitely not one of them. I found a correlation between my desire to work (which was related to my faith, and my hope), and the consistency with which I had powerful prayer and meaningful scripture study.

Did I still get down and depressed? Of course. But as long as I was doing my very best to fulfill those two commandments, I could stay on track and on target. I would have a desire to work, to serve, to lead, to grow, and to go and do the things the Lord had commanded. The blessings promised to those who keep these commandments are crucial for those struggling with depression, as those blessings include an abundance of hope. I also found that when I chose to fast in addition to reading the scriptures and praying, the results were absolutely incredible!

I feel it is important to note that my scripture study had to be focused on things that really mattered to me, and that I had to make an effort to apply what I learned from them. A casual couple of minutes spent skimming the chapter headings was not sufficient for my needs. I needed to replenish my hope bucket by drawing deeply from the well of life, and that required effort.

Similarly, my prayers were most effective when they were well thought out and not repetitious; I would go over the events of the day and ask questions, admit and confess mistakes I had made that day, and really try to make each prayer meaningful. It seemed difficult at first, but I found that over time, it became a habit, and for my efforts, I was blessed with solace and strength during difficult times throughout my mission.

Obeying the commandments to pray and study the scriptures will help you remain in control over the darkness that would taint your attitude. Study and prayer will also allow you to feel more in charge of your destiny, both here on earth and throughout eternity. Try it for a week, and I guarantee you that, depressed or not, your attitude will be improved. But remember, it is important to read and pray every day; otherwise, the water in the hope bucket runs low, and it's difficult to get motivated when you're looking at having to refill the entire bucket.

In my experience, reading the scriptures and praying are, without a doubt, the fundamental building blocks that allowed me to survive clinical depression and obtain a measure of joy from my work as a missionary. And I believe these blessings are available to all who diligently fulfill these commandments, regardless of their circumstances.

EIGHT

I will prepare the way before you—1 Nephi 17:13

So what is the role of medication in all of this? Perhaps you are among the many who feel that surely the Lord will lift this burden from you if you pray with enough faith or receive a priesthood blessing. And while I do believe that miracles of healing can and do occur, I also have a strong testimony, based on personal experience, that these miracles cannot and will not come about until we have done everything in our own power to treat our ailments.

The first fifteen months of my mission were the hardest months of my life. In addition to the normal rigors of the missionary lifestyle, one of the greatest challenges facing the elders and sisters in my mission was severe and widespread disobedience that robbed us of much of the Spirit that we otherwise would have been entitled to. As a new missionary I was taught by my peers that "success," as they termed it, was not contingent upon personal obedience or the Spirit of God.

The only person I felt I could trust was my first mission president, and so my relationship with him was precious to me. When severe medical conditions necessitated his release, I remember weeping and feeling like I was losing the only real friend I had made since entering the field. Extenuating circumstances would lead to my serving under five different mission presidents by the time I finished my mission. I remember going through each change in leadership feeling more and more forgotten, alone, and unwanted than before.

These trials, combined with my depression, dealt severe blows to my faith. I became a jaded, cynical elder with a devil-may-care attitude toward my mission. It was at this point of dire need that I first received word of my mother's remarkable recovery resulting from her new medication.

My initial reaction was understandably skeptical. After all, it wasn't uncommon for my mother's perpetual valley of depression to be punctuated by occasional peaks of mania. However, as weeks went by and I continued to hear more about my mother's transformed attitude and its apparent consistency over time, a ray of hope crept into my weary psyche.

I was taking medication at the time, but I think anyone who spent time with me for an extended period would attest to the fact that my medication was only partially successful in helping me to fend off my depression. I had notorious mood swings, and it was all I could do to muster the faith to get out of bed in the morning. I felt that my circumstances had cheated me out of the mission I had hoped for fifteen months earlier—that there was nothing I could do to change things.

Trying a new medication changed all that. The pains and aches I seemed to constantly feel soon vanished. My moods became more consistent, predictable, and productive. Most importantly, I finally felt as if I could choose how to feel toward my circumstances, whereas before it had seemed as if I had no choice but to dread them. I had gained attitude control.

I began to view my unusual mission experiences not as curses, but as unique opportunities to learn and grow. This attitude of adaptability and gratitude would serve me well as I faced the same challenges that seemed so insurmountable prior to my new medicine. Did the medication make my trials disappear? No, but it let me charge them head-on with a smile on my face and a song in my heart, and that made all the difference.

There were several brief points during my mission when I felt close enough to the Lord that I could barely feel the effects of my clinical depression; these always came during periods of fasting, study, prayer, and service. This may sound like I am claiming that if someone is righteous enough, he or she will not need medication. While I do believe that the Lord will bless us greatly as we try to become closer to Him, I also believe it's foolish to embrace this mentality—the mentality that righteous living will make our illnesses and trials disappear.

I say this for two reasons. First, this life is intended to be a time of trying and testing. A loving Father in Heaven knows we need trials to grow. Second, even if righteous living could guarantee respite from our trials, you and I will eventually make a mistake. We are human; we are weak, and we will fail. And when you suffer from clinical depression, like I do, you dwell on even the smallest of failures, and when you do, you fall into a cycle of despair, self-pity, and apathy. In your mind, you feel like it is impossible for you to break out. And while it *is* possible to break free of these cycles, it's true that it is *always* time-consuming to do so, because sincere change does not occur overnight.

To make a long story short, proper medication has allowed me—and will allow you—to have greater hope in the Savior and His teachings than you were able to before. This is because your attitude toward those teachings and life in general will be more positive and energetic.

It is possible to cope with clinical depression without medication, but I believe we should only attempt to handle the illness in this manner until we are able to obtain healing through a combination of spiritual and chemical remedies. I do not believe that there is any righteous excuse for choosing not to seek professional help and medication for clinical depression. What it boils down to is whether or not we are humble enough to admit we need help.

Additionally, please do not justify or excuse yourself by saying that the money would be better spent elsewhere. Proper medication will improve every aspect of not only your own life, but of the lives of those with whom you associate. Pridefully refraining from seeking help will only result in your continually draining the hope of those whom you most love. Never stop searching or working toward a treatment that works for your specific needs. Do not try to excuse or justify yourself by waiting for the Lord to heal you or tell you how to be healed. In his day, Captain Moroni strongly rebuked those who had this attitude: "Behold, could ye suppose that ye could sit upon your thrones, and because of the exceeding goodness of God ye could do nothing and he would deliver you? Behold, if ye have supposed this ye have supposed in vain" (Alma 60:11).

I invite you with all the energy of my heart to seek for both spiritual and physical treatment to overcome the grave plague of depression, which robs its victims of hope, faith, and joy. I plead with you to look to the Lord and live, and by so doing, endure to the end. You were not sent to this earth to fail. You were not sent here to cower before the adversary and his diabolic minions. You were not sent here to be miserable. You were sent here to have joy.

"Adam fell that men might be; and men are, that they might have joy" (2 Nephi 2:25).

I testify that God will help you in this endeavor as you do your best to follow Him in faith: ". . . for I know that the Lord giveth no commandments unto the children of men, save he shall prepare a way for them that they may accomplish the thing which he commandeth them" (1 Nephi 3:7).

The way to lasting hope and joy may not be easy, but it is possible, and it is worth it. You are a child of God, and He will *never* forsake you or forget you. In fact, I invite you to get down on your knees right now and ask Heavenly Father Himself if He loves you and if He will help you to survive your trials.

I know He will answer your prayers. I know this because He answered the prayers of a lost, confused, bitter, and angry nineteen-year-old boy. That night in April 2004, I didn't see anything in my life worth redeeming or loving, but the Lord did. As I prayed, He told me so. He spoke peace to my tortured soul and embraced me in the arms of His everlasting love. Life will never be easy, but with the knowledge of His love for you, it will become more bearable. I leave that promise with you in the name of Jesus Christ, amen.

PART THREE
DAVID'S STORY

NINE

Charity suffereth long—Moroni 7:45

To begin, let me speak briefly about what this book is and what it is not. This is an account of how three people dealt with a serious illness. Most instances of depression do not last as long as G.G.'s did. Neither is most depression as severe as what she and Greg experienced. This book doesn't intend to make generalizations about depression or provide a comprehensive overview that addresses all of its symptoms and consequences. I am not a doctor; I am only a witness.

While we are talking about a single illness and three specific people, the lessons we've learned extend beyond those particulars and, I hope, will be helpful to others experiencing severe and extended trials of different types. We have been specific in our commentary because we would like those who are dealing with trials to both understand and feel understood. And to hold onto hope. If we included only abstract and general principles gained from our experiences without including some of the details, I believe our stories would not resonate as deeply and would be less useful in the lives of others.

It is unwise to compare crosses, and I do not mean to do so as I recount my experiences. I cannot say that my suffering was greater or less than another person's, because I cannot truly understand how anyone else's trials have afflicted them. Only our God and our loving Savior can truly understand such things. I can simply say that my trials were very difficult for me, difficult enough to drive me to my knees with the most fervent prayers I have ever uttered. These trials changed me in a deep and permanent way.

Ours is a sad story with a happy ending. Some may say, "This doesn't apply to me because my story doesn't have a happy ending." My response to that is, "Then you're not at the end of your story yet." After one year, my story with G.G. did not have a happy ending. It didn't after two years, nor did it after three, five, or ten years. In the fifteenth and twentieth years, I would have emphatically said that my story did not have a happy ending. It was only after the possibility of having a happy ending had nearly vanished from my hopes that the happy ending came.

One of the most fundamental promises of the Atonement is that there will be a happy ending to each of our stories if we will take the steps required of us. In His infinite wisdom, the Lord, who knows all ends from their beginnings, seldom reveals the precise timing or details of our happy ending to us. However, because of His love for us and the sacrifice that proved this love forever, we can trust that those happy endings will come.

We have used our specific stories to testify that the Atonement is real—very real. The Atonement does not work only in general terms; it works for the specific, nasty details of terribly difficult problems and deep despair. Our Savior suffered and died to save individuals from their own sins and to strengthen each of us during the minutes and days and years of our greatest challenges.

The sky was dark when He was crucified, and the tomb was dark when His body was placed in it. But on the third day, the sun rose— and so did He. And so will we.

The Shark and the Storm

It is difficult to communicate the experience of passing through a very long trial. Each day is difficult, but the cumulative effect of facing challenges day after day magnifies the burden. When climbing a high mountain, our first steps don't feel that hard. As we continue to climb, however, all of the steps that came before make each additional step a little more difficult. If someone who didn't know what the earlier parts of the climb were like were to see us as we neared the summit, they would likely conclude that we weren't very strong climbers because of the weariness in our steps, when just the opposite would be true.

So how does one write about an extended time of trial? I could truthfully describe each day. Such a description might begin with, "This was a very hard day," followed by the details of the difficulties. The next description would begin, "This was a very hard day," and again relate the familiar or new trials of that day. After fifty or sixty such descriptions, a change might occur, and the passage would begin, "This was not as hard a day as yesterday was," followed by a discussion of some small improvement in G.G.'s illness. But then the next day's story would begin, "This was a very hard day."

After a hundred such accounts, the book would begin to be tedious. Before I described a thousand days, most readers would give up. No one would read about three thousand or six thousand or nine thousand such days. A story like this would be too discouraging, and the repetitive recitation of the same struggles would quickly become unappealing. The reader would think, "Why does this have to continue for so long? Can't the author find something positive to talk about? Why doesn't anything good ever happen?"

Precisely.

I believe a metaphorical description is the only way to effectively portray the experience of living with and trying to help a severely depressed person for many years.

When G.G. and I married, I was a new member of the Church. We had dated for some time prior to my baptism and were counseled by our bishop to be married civilly and then be sealed after we had been married for a year. This would not have been appropriate advice for some couples, but it was right for us. My family, none of whom were or are members, attended and enjoyed our civil ceremony, and after a year had passed, we were sealed in the Los Angeles Temple.

And so we set out in our little boat in a new marriage upon a broad and inviting sea. The sky was blue, and the sun was shining. Seagulls wheeled above us. We plotted our course so that we would sail safely, avoiding the rocks and reefs that lay waiting for sailors who were not careful where they sailed. We determined that we would strive to obey the commandments and follow the promptings of the Spirit. Our little craft was pointed toward the celestial kingdom. It would be a long trip, but we knew we could arrive at our destination if we followed the course we had planned.

For some time, our trip proceeded as expected. As with any long ocean voyage, squalls blew across the sea, but our boat was sound. We secured the hatches, sent a storm sail aloft, and were able to pass through the short rainstorms without any damage. After the storms passed, we checked our map, took new bearings, and proceeded toward our goal.

At times, our course took us on a track through uncharted waters we hadn't expected to pass through. We watched carefully for obstacles and were able to pass through those waters with no injury to our little craft or ourselves. It was not difficult to remember that Heavenly Father was watching over us and guiding us past any danger as we moved toward our intended destination.

Then, on a day that began like others that had preceded it, we saw ominous clouds on the horizon. A low rumble of thunder carried across the sea, and the waves began to rise. We had seen such weather signs before; however, we thought we were prepared to ride out the short storm.

As we made our normal preparations for heavy weather, I saw, for the first time, a large shark in the distance. Its fin broke through the surface of the water and proceeded powerfully forward, splitting the water, then disappearing back into the ocean. I could not determine how large the shark was, nor did I know where it had come from or the direction it was headed.

The storm bore down upon us. The waves were small at first, but as the wind increased in velocity, the waves grew larger. I reminded myself that although our boat was small, it was strong, and G.G. and I had weathered other storms. Sometimes those storms had been uncomfortable, and some had lasted longer than we would have liked, but we had survived them all.

· But the storm grew even more powerful. Strong gusts of wind buffeted us, and the sky grew darker and darker. Suddenly, the rain came in sheets of almost solid water. The sound of the wind was unlike anything I had heard before as it drove the rain remorselessly against our sail. Large waves lifted the little boat higher and higher and then slammed it back down. The wind whipped off the tops of the waves and pounded us with dark ocean water.

I had never experienced a storm this severe. There was an ominous danger here I had never encountered. Not once had I worried that our boat might not survive a storm. I looked for some sign that the tempest was weakening, but there was no light in any direction.

I did not think the waves could get any larger, but they did. G.G. and I held on as tightly as we could as wave after wave smashed down on our boat as if trying to drive us beneath the water. Pieces of our craft began to break off and disappear into the darkness. Then our mast snapped and our sail was blown away by the howling wind.

After what seemed like an eternity, the wind began to ease, and the violent ocean waves slowly subsided. Bit by bit, it became lighter, and I could see again. But our boat was in disrepair; I did not see how it could ever sail again.

Then I looked toward G.G. She was seriously injured, weak, and bleeding from several deep cuts. I tried to stop the bleeding, but it continued. I did not know what I could do.

I glanced up and saw the shark's fin again, much closer this time. Below the water's surface, I could see its indistinct, dark form. The shark must have been drawn by the scent of G.G.'s blood dripping into the water. It swam in slow circles around our boat.

I turned back to G.G. and applied every bandage I could find to her wounds, layer upon layer, winding them as tightly as I could. Finally, when I thought I had stopped the bleeding, she fell asleep.

I was then able to inspect our boat. There were many repairs to be made, and I didn't know if I had the knowledge necessary to complete all of them. I worked on the boat for hours. I stopped to rest for a moment and to think about how we could get back to the course we had been following. As I looked across the sea, I saw more towering, dark clouds on the horizon.

I did not think it was possible, but the second storm was worse than the first. The giant waves and wind quickly destroyed my repairs. Much of the equipment that had helped us survive the first storm was lost to the ocean, and I could do little to minimize the storm's effects on the boat. Wave after wave pounded down on the deck. At times, the ocean's power drove our craft beneath the water, and it struggled to bring itself back to the surface. I could not steer or exert any control over the boat. It required all of my strength just to hang on and not be swept overboard.

Finally, this storm also lifted, and by some miracle, I was still alive. I was exhausted, and I looked over to where G.G. lay. She was bleeding from new cuts, and her bandages were soaked with bright red blood. I thought of the shark and looked up in time to see it dive beneath the boat. I could feel a bump as it passed underneath.

I quickly searched the broken boat for something I could use as a bandage. A few pieces of clothing remained. I squeezed as much sea water from them as possible and tied them around G.G.'s cuts.

No more clouds appeared on the horizon. I thought I saw a ship or two steaming in the far distance and hoped for rescue, but they soon disappeared. The storm had taken most of our drinking water, so we only had a few sips. Soon we became terribly thirsty. Day after day, the sun hung in the sky, a giant fireball that burned down on us.

The boat was broken in so many ways that I did not think it could ever sail again. Any thoughts of resuming our original course of travel dwindled. All my energy was consumed with the task of merely surviving until the sun set, and I could sleep.

The shark was never far away now. It would dive only to resurface a few minutes later. It cruised by the boat on one side, then on the other, scraping its rough skin against the hull.

One day as the sun blazed in the sky, the shark began to bump the boat. Again and again, harder and harder it hit our boat. We began to rock back and forth. I grabbed onto a handhold. The shark wouldn't stop. I turned to see G.G. slip over the side of the boat into the water.

I scrambled over to where she had fallen. I could see her just below the surface. She was not moving. I reached down to grab her hand to pull her up, but my grip was weak, and her hand slipped from mine. I clutched for it again, and again she slipped away. I knew the shark was close.

G.G. sank farther down into the ocean, and I could no longer reach her from the boat. I dived into the water and swam down to find her. At first I could not see her, but I kept swimming and finally located her in the murky darkness. I put one arm around her and pulled with the other toward the surface. Slowly and with great effort, we rose back up toward the light.

When my head broke the surface, I gasped for breath. G.G. looked very pale and was barely breathing. How could I lift her out of the water? As I desperately searched for something I could use to help get her back into the boat, I saw the shark's head for the first time. I saw nothing but dead, black eyes and row upon row of terrifying teeth.

I turned back toward the boat, frantic to find a way so, G.G. slipped from my grasp. I saw her descending sl darkness again.

Again I went down after her. I was so tired. I could see her down below me, dropping ever farther. I swam and swam and finally, reaching as far down as I could, I touched her, then held her. I looked up. The surface was so far away. I wanted to breathe so badly. With what little strength remained, I took a stroke toward the surface, but I hardly seemed to move.

Then the shark brushed against my leg in the darkness.

I was convinced beyond all doubt that I was powerless, that nothing I could do would have any effect. Disaster seemed unavoidable. It was then that the Lord caught me up into the light. In an instant, G.G. and I were out of the water. The storm and the shark vanished. The battle that had consumed most of our adult lives was over. Through His grace, the Lord had allowed us to overcome.

I use a storm and a shark as analogies for several reasons. For me, at times, G.G.'s depression seemed like a great impersonal, external force that tossed us back and forth emotionally. It seemed that just as G.G. would move past a time when her illness was more severe, and the waters would appear to calm, I could sense emotional storm clouds gathering on the horizon. I would again hear a distant thunder and feel that there was nothing I could do to prevent the coming deluge.

The shark is apt for this analogy as well because at other times the illness seemed malignant and very personal. Her illness could also strike without warning, unlike the storm we could see gathering in the distance. Satan often uses the trials in our lives to slash at our testimonies and cut us away from our faith so that we feel isolated and alone. At these times, Satan feels like a very individual enemy, crafting darts to skewer us at our weakest points

However, when the storm was gone and the shark disappeared, I was able to look back over the experience with a clearer view than I had while I was in the midst of the fight. As the challenges rained down on us, I frequently felt the assistance and strength of the Lord, but then another wave would break over me and I could think of nothing but fighting for our lives. With the clearer view came an even greater appreciation for all the times and all the ways the Lord had protected me, even while I was buffeted by great forces.

As I have thought back through all the years and all the experiences, I realize more clearly that He was always there. The Spirit would gently point out the tender mercies of the Lord that were real and invaluable but which I had failed to notice. I know now that instead of carrying me a thousand times, he carried me a million times.

Through my experiences, I have also learned many important things about supporting and helping a loved one with this illness. I have learned greater compassion, patience, and love. And I have learned several key principles. I would like to suggest three things to remember as you extend your hand to support a loved one suffering from depression:

1. Persist in wanting to help, and continue to seek Heavenly Father's help to maintain your motivation and desire to help.
2. Learn about depression; otherwise, you will likely come to the wrong conclusions about many of the things you observe.
3. Understand that you need the Savior.

WANTING TO HELP

The statement that you must first *want* to help your loved one who is suffering from depression may strike some as odd. "Of course I want to help," you say. "What kind of a person do you think I am?" However, because of the nature of severe and extended depression, this illness not only affects those who suffer from it, but those who love and are trying to support them. Discouragement and despair take their toll on the helper as well. Thus it is critical that you firmly decide that you want to help and that you ask for Heavenly Father's support in this endeavor. Satan can be very effective at amplifying the hopelessness you will likely feel when your efforts to help seem to produce little fruit. At times, you may feel drained of any ability to help and be tempted to believe that anything you try is bound to fail. It's a short step from feeling like you are completely powerless to losing the desire to continue offering help.

Because of the toll taken on the loved ones of individuals suffering from depression, it is not unusual for the husband or wife of a depressed person to seek divorce. While it's impossible to judge such a situation, I often wonder if at least some of these ruptures occur because the non-depressed spouse cannot maintain his or her desire to help long enough.

The spouse thinks about how his or her life is turning out to be different than he or she had planned. Their companion seems to have been replaced by someone much different than the person they married. They may think, *Perhaps the marriage was a mistake. It's just too hard. Surely this is not the life God intended for me.* Eventually, discouragement overwhelms the desire to help.

When someone in your family is severely depressed, your life changes from what you expected it to be to what the Lord, in His infinite wisdom, wants your life to be. For most, it is a surprising trial, one you thought would surely never come to you. However, if you experienced the depression of a family member or friend earlier in your life, perhaps this was the trial you feared the most.

Why would the Lord allow this? Because He loves you. Why would your loved one be asked to suffer like they do? Because He loves them, too.

A member of our ward whose wife has fought a debilitating chronic illness for many years once offered me an insight about our shared experience. He said, "Our wives will get us into the celestial kingdom. Without them, we might not make it."

As we look at the wide array of experiences that occur in the lives of righteous people everywhere, we may wonder if, within that incredible variety, there is a common thread, a shared direction that makes it possible for each of these people to return to Heavenly Father. At times, in moments of weakness, we may look at the lives of others and think, "Everything always works out well for them. They're not suffering like my family and I are."

Of course, the reply to this statement is that we don't truly understand the experiences of those people. We don't know their secret demons. We don't fully understand their past, and we certainly can't see their future. We can, however, rest assured that they are being tested and tried in all the ways that Heavenly Father knows are necessary for them. Our particular tests may be different from those of others, but we are all tested.

In a general conference address, Elder Boyd K. Packer spoke about our varied trials and experiences:

> Some are tested by poor health, some by a body that is deformed or homely. Others are tested by handsome

and healthy bodies; some by the passion of youth; others by the erosions of age.

Some suffer disappointment in marriage, family problems; others live in poverty and obscurity. Some (perhaps this is the hardest test) find ease and luxury.

All are part of the test, and there is more equality in this testing than sometimes we suspect. (Boyd K. Packer, "The Choice," *Ensign,* November 1980, 20)

A wise friend of mine who has suffered enormous health trials of her own told me that she often repeated to herself the phrase, "This life is the test, not the reward." Some Latter-day Saints seem to believe, at least subconsciously, that obedience to the gospel will prevent major trials from happening to them. These people are uneasy with the idea that someone could be adhering to all the commandments and still have serious, even life-threatening difficulties. While we certainly can bring upon ourselves a wide range of problems through our failure to live the commandments, some trials will happen in spite of all we are doing right.

Peter explains, "Beloved, think it not strange concerning the fiery trial which is to try you, as though some strange thing happened unto you" (1 Peter 4:12).

Consider the life of Joseph Smith, who was certainly beloved of the Lord. Did Heavenly Father spare Joseph his Liberty Jail experience because Joseph paid his tithing? Was Joseph able to avoid being beaten and tarred because he faithfully offered heartfelt prayers? It would have been so easy for Heavenly Father to intervene and to allow Joseph to steer clear of Carthage Jail, but Carthage happened despite the fact that Joseph followed heavenly guidance throughout his life.

Have you or I earned more favor with the Lord than Joseph Smith through greater faith and obedience? If someday we are privileged to sit down with Joseph and Moses, Peter, and Paul, Nephi, and Alma and Mormon and Moroni in the celestial kingdom, will we really belong in their company if we have not walked some miles on a rocky road? Eternal life is not for wimps.

Success in this life does not come from avoiding serious trials and tests. Success is found in responding well to those trials that do come. Our mortal lives are a place and time of testing; the great reward for righteous living and overcoming all things by faith will come afterward.

When you wonder whether you have the strength to continue helping a family member or friend with depression, take a moment to remember that this mortal life is only a tiny slice of eternal life. Our lives before our mortal birth go back further than we can possibly imagine, and they will extend forever after our mortal bodies expire.

And yet, despite the brevity of this earth life, everything we do here is vital, essential, and determinative of the kind of life we will enjoy after we leave this earth. The depressed person, who on earth may bring you so much despair, will leave his or her illness behind in a mortal body. The greatest test of that person's life may be this depression and, if they endure that test to the best of their abilities, they may—with the Atonement of Christ—have done all that is necessary to enter the celestial kingdom.

One of your greatest tests, the one you get graded on, may well be how you respond to the depressed man, woman, teenager, or child you love. The person who causes you so much frustration and anguish and tears may, in fact, be placed in your life by Heavenly Father as a way of providing you with a chance for your greatest blessings. I have learned that some of our most significant opportunities come heavily disguised. You may have passed all the quizzes and midterms of mortality only to be given a final examination that shows your Savior how much you love Him by the way you serve one of His terribly wounded sheep.

As we read in the Doctrine and Covenants, "My son, peace be unto thy soul; thine adversity and thine afflictions shall be but a small moment; And then, if thou endure it well, God shall exalt thee on high; thou shalt triumph over all thy foes" (121:7–8).

That—being exalted on high—is why you want to help this person.

UNDERSTANDING DEPRESSION

One of the great challenges for a depressed person is the fact that most people simply don't understand what is going on in that person's mind and body.

Well-meaning family and friends who have never dealt with depression suggest a wide range of solutions that are typically way off the mark. These friends and family members draw on experiences when they have felt blue for a few days and then felt better. This is not depression. The remedy that worked for them almost certainly will not work for someone who suffers from this illness. For longer than I care to remember, I was one of those well-meaning people when it came to dealing with G.G.'s depression. I had many great solutions. Unfortunately, they were all for the wrong problems. Following are some of the things that I learned about depression, through my experiences with G.G.

* * *

One of the most difficult challenges for a faithful member of the Church who is depressed is that it is very difficult for him or her to feel the Spirit. A wonderful conference talk, a tremendous testimony meeting, a great temple session, or a beautiful priesthood blessing can leave this person untouched and unmoved, while everyone around them seems to feel an outpouring of the Spirit.

Is the Spirit present at those occasions? Yes. Can the Spirit help the depressed person? Of course. Does depression remove any of the Spirit's power? No. But can the depressed person always feel and understand the Spirit when it is present? Not necessarily.

The nature of depression often causes depressed people to blame themselves for their spiritual isolation. They believe they are bad people and that they must have done something very wrong because they can't feel the Spirit. They believe the falsehood that depression is a moral failure.

It can be difficult for depressed people and their loved ones to accept that this illness can sometimes interfere with the delicate spiritual receptors that allow other faithful Saints to feel the promptings of the Holy Ghost. This is because, typically, these receptors are damaged by breaking commandments related to the use of improper substances or violating the law of chastity. However, mental illness can also damage those receptors in an innocent, righteous person.

I first learned this information from a counselor with LDS Family Services. He was making a presentation about depression for a bishop's council during the early stages of G.G.'s depression, which was in the early 1980s. He explained that depression sometimes made it very difficult for his patients to feel or hear the Holy Ghost and described this as one of the greatest burdens that accompanied this illness.

* * *

I've also learned that depression changes the way a person perceives reality. It injects emotions and overtones into a situation that a healthy individual would not experience in the same circumstances. When a depressed person tells you he sees an event or a situation in a much different way than you do, he's not confused or foolish or lying or dramatizing. He is describing what he truly sees and feels. The difference between his view and yours is caused by his disease. In fact, if he said that he saw and felt things the same way that you did, he would sometimes be lying.

Someone who has always enjoyed good mental health may find it difficult to comprehend that the way he or she sees and feels and remembers experiences is largely the result of a complex series of minute chemical reactions and processes that are occurring at lighting speed in our brains. If those chemical processes are in balance, a person may perceive a sacrament service as an enjoyable, uplifting experience. However, if those chemical processes are not working properly, the same person may perceive the same sacrament service as an unending condemnation of their numerous failings and deficiencies, and the people in attendance may be seen as threatening and uncomprehending.

It is important to remember that these chemical processes are part of our mortal bodies, *not* our spirits. We have each known spiritual giants trapped in bodies that manifest a wide range of physical limitations and illnesses. With the right spiritual eyes, we can learn to discern that spiritual giants may also be trapped in bodies that manifest a wide range of mental and emotional limitations and illnesses. All bodies, no matter their condition, house the spirit children of heavenly parents.

Our bodies are made of the elements of this fallen earth. None of our bodies work perfectly—otherwise we wouldn't die. Each of us has a variety of problems that originate within our bodies. Those whom we call healthy may have physical problems that manifest themselves much later in their mortal lives. And some, including those who are depressed, have serious physical problems that manifest themselves much earlier.

* * *

Another symptom of severe depression is repeated thoughts of suicide. When these thoughts arise, a faithful Latter-day Saint is particularly distressed. He or she knows that suicide is wrong, but the thoughts keep coming back into his or her mind uninvited. For a severely depressed man or woman, suicide can also appear to be a way to end the intense and unremitting pain of this illness.

Please do not ignore suicidal statements. Ever.

It is difficult for some people to understand how depression can be labeled a life-threatening illness, because a depressed person's body does not appear to be deteriorating or suffering. But the way depression takes a life is via suicide.

There is no reliable formula for what you should say or do when your loved one is suicidal, but I can tell you that you need to talk to them, and keep them talking for a long time. The Spirit will help you. You must be prepared to take the depressed person to the emergency room or to a psychiatric hospital for his or her own safety if you receive any indication whatsoever that he or she might act on their suicidal thoughts. When in doubt, go to the hospital.

* * *

Throughout the years, I have learned from my son, Greg, who also suffered from depression, that depressed teenagers present some unique challenges. The first is discovering that the problem exists. The teenage years often represent an emotional roller-coaster ride, even for healthy kids, so it's easy for parents to overlook the signs of depression.

Parents want their children to be healthy. After experiencing G.G.'s depression, I did not want Greg to have the same illness, so I minimized the symptoms and attributed them to Greg's difficulty with two moves in four years. When I talked with him individually, I tried to cheer him up and encourage him. And although there was nothing wrong with doing this, it was not a substitute for getting him the help he really needed. I was blind to the illness that had been so readily apparent to me in the sons and daughters of others.

However, G.G. recognized what I did not and tried to persuade Greg to accept counseling. He was obedient enough to go but resistant enough that the counseling did not do him much good. We tried medication, and I saw what I wanted to see, thinking that he was improving when he was not. He refused to talk about how he was really feeling, and I wanted to take that silence as an indication of the absence of a problem.

Fortunately—very fortunately—the Lord was attentive when I was not. Miracles occurred, which allowed him to serve a mission. An outstanding bishop worked long and hard with Greg so he would be ready. A stake president listened to the Spirit and took extraordinary steps that permitted Greg to receive a mission call earlier than would otherwise have been the case. Greg entered the MTC at the right time; a delay might have led him to give up on the idea that he could ever be a missionary.

Step by step, the Lord helped Greg find motivation and relief as he gave his all and served an honorable mission. As you have read earlier in this book, he rose to a great challenge and because of his illness, he had further to climb than other missionaries did. However, Greg found a great deal of healing as he worked hard and did his best to stay close to the His Father in Heaven.

I have learned a great deal from my son. The following are a few of the signs that may indicate your teenager is suffering from depression. It is important to remember, however, that someone can be depressed without showing all of these signs. Doctors typically recommend that if a person exhibits several of these signs over a period of more than two weeks, especially if the behavior comes on suddenly, the help of a doctor should be sought:

1. Outbursts of anger that are disproportionate to the provocation
2. Difficulty in making or keeping friends
3. Associating with friends who seem depressed
4. Spending extended periods of time alone
5. Making statements such as, "I wish I was dead" or "I could die and nobody would care."

6. A significant drop in school grades
7. Expressions of concern from teachers, parents of friends, etc. about the teenager
8. Changes in sleep patterns, such as sleeping all the time or insomnia
9. A loss of interest in friends or activities that the teenager formerly enjoyed
10. Significant weight loss, including anorexia or bulimia (often a particular problem for girls) or significant weight gain
11. A significant preoccupation with violence in various forms or repeated involvement with pornography (often a particular problem for boys)
12. Victimization by bullies in school or elsewhere
13. Significant changes in personal grooming—e.g., a formerly neat person becomes sloppy
14. A loss of commitment to living the gospel and attending Church meetings and activities

Since most teenagers desperately want to fit in and not be "different," it can be very difficult to persuade them to acknowledge that they have a problem or to accept professional help. This is a time for parental persistence and loving persuasion, rather than loud commands. Forced cooperation may result in passive-aggression that could undermine the beneficial effects of treatment. Just as it took me a long time to accept that Greg had a problem, it took him a long time to do so as well. A parent cannot force this type of self-discovery.

* * *

There are two classes of professional help that can be a resource for someone suffering from depression:

1) Medical doctors (usually psychiatrists)
2) Therapists or counselors (usually psychologists)

Sometimes the same person may perform the role of both medical doctor and counselor, but usually this is not the case. It is also important to realize that your first experience with a psychiatrist or therapist may not be a positive one; you may need to make a change. Sometimes the personality or training of a particular person may not fit your needs. It's not easy, but you need to keep trying.

Some Latter-day Saints are very opposed to seeking help from psychiatrists and psychologists on principle. However, I'm not certain what principle—especially what gospel principle—they have in mind. If someone were to break a leg, no one would think of telling them to simply get a priesthood blessing, think nice thoughts, and exert their faith in lieu of taking them to a doctor to get the broken bone properly set. This is not to say that help from a psychiatrist or psychologist should replace prayer and blessings. Both the temporal and spiritual must work together. The old saying "pray like everything depends on God and work like everything depends on you" applies well to mental illnesses. The "work" includes taking the sick person to medical professionals who can help him.

In order to obtain medication for his illness, a depressed person will need to see a physician who can prescribe that medication. The good news about medication for depression is that it has improved immensely over the last twenty-five years. The bad news is that it's not perfect yet.

One of the challenges medical professionals treating depression face is selecting the right medication from a wide range of possibilities. Inevitably, even for the most skilled physician, there is an element of trial and error involved in selecting medications. The first medicine may not work, and the patient may need to try another. In some cases, a combination of two or more medications is needed. Praying for your doctor, asking the Lord to guide him or her in treating your loved one, is always an excellent practice.

Trying out different medications is typically a very difficult experience for the depressed person. He sees a ray of hope only to have that hope dashed when a medication doesn't work. It is also important to be aware that some types of medication take time to reach their full potential, so the patient may have to take the pills from two to six weeks before discovering that they aren't working. One of your jobs is to encourage the depressed person to keep going back to their doctor if the prescribed medicine is not doing its job.

Be aware that antidepressants are powerful drugs that can have negative side effects for certain people. Sometimes the medication may seem to be working for the depression, but the patient can't tolerate the side effects. A trip back to the doctor is needed. A different drug in the same general family of drugs may provide the benefits without the side effects. In some cases, a second drug may be able to control the side effects.

An entirely new challenge can arise when the medication *does* work. Sometimes people suffering from depression will feel so much better after taking medication that they will be convinced that a permanent healing has taken place. Therefore, they don't feel the need to take their medicine anymore. In a matter of days, a crash will occur, and the emotional whiplash they experience will often be worse than the depression alone was. Encourage your loved one to keep taking her pills until her doctor tells her differently. Know that even when going off a particular medication *is* advised, it must be done in a particular manner to avoid a crash.

Someone who has been depressed for an extended period of time will also need a therapist, someone who can spend time talking to them. Depressed people often develop unhealthy thinking patterns and coping strategies to help them get through their difficult days and weeks. These habits may interfere with their recovery, even if the medication is working.

A good therapist can help someone suffering from depression by identifying these destructive thinking patterns and leading the patient to healthier, more effective ways of dealing with problems. Negative habits are often hard to eliminate, so one visit to a therapist will probably not be enough.

While there are skilled therapists of all faiths, in our experience, a good LDS therapist is very helpful. During the course of therapy, the fundamental beliefs and values of a patient a play key role. An active LDS therapist may be better able to understand the important role the gospel plays in the lives and decisions of LDS patients more readily than one who is not familiar with these beliefs. Unfortunately, LDS therapists are difficult or impossible to find in some regions. LDS Family Services can help you locate either an LDS therapist or a non-LDS therapist who works well with LDS patients.

* * *

Cost can be an issue with medical treatments. Under the health insurance laws of many states, treatment options for mental illness are

limited. An annual coverage limitation on the number of visits to a therapist is common. You will want to become familiar with the mental-illness
coverage offered by your health insurance.

If you receive health insurance through your employer, know that
you will need to be careful in the event that you change jobs. A gap in
insurance coverage may result in a waiting period before pre-existing
medical conditions, including mental illness, will be covered under your
new insurance. In some circumstances, it may be financially advisable to
take advantage of COBRA coverage[1] under your previous employer's
insurance plan for a period of time until the new insurance becomes
effective. Check with the person in your company who handles employee
insurance benefits for details.

At times, people will avoid obtaining needed medical treatment
for depression due to financial considerations. Without health insurance—and sometimes even with health insurance—medical costs can
be daunting. However, avoiding or terminating treatment for serious
depression in the face of financial constraints can have grave consequences. Remember, depression is a potentially fatal disease.

When I was a bishop, I was always happy to use fast offering funds to
help treat all serious illnesses, including mental illness, when the family
was unable to cover all the costs with their own resources. If payment for
treatment is a problem, see your bishop. When the members of the
Church make their fast offering contributions, they expect those contributions to be used to help members in need. Financial assistance from
fast offerings is never treated as a loan that must be paid back, but if you
desire, you can always make generous fast offering contributions when
your financial condition improves.

---

[1] COBRA (Consolidated Omnibus Budget Reconciliation Act) was a federal law estab-
lished in 1985, that requires most employers with group health plans to offer employees
the opportunity to temporarily continue their group health care coverage under their
employer's plan if their coverage would otherwise cease due to termination, layoff, or
other change in employment status. The employee must pay insurance premiums
without any employer contribution, but coverage is guaranteed regardless of prior health
problems. Premiums, calculated under group pricing plans, are usually less expensive
than an individual policy. An employee can typically continue this coverage for eighteen
months, although additional time may be available under some circumstances.

* * *

Understanding, compassion, and medical care for depression are vital. It is inexcusable to deny a seriously depressed person proper care and support. We would never allow someone with a broken leg to lie untended in the street or advise a person with cancer to simply think nice thoughts. We remember Christ's story of the Good Samaritan in which first the lofty priest and then the self-regarding Levite "passed by on the other side" (Luke 10:31–32). When we neglect the wounds of another, whether mental or physical, or when we hide in our own ignorance, we are passing by on the other side and putting ourselves in the company of those who do not live their religion.

Relying on the Savior

"O Lord, I have trusted in thee, and I will trust in thee forever" (2 Nephi 4:34).

At its worst, depression can make you feel like your loved one has died or has been replaced by someone you do not know. The spark that once motivated them and made them unique seems to have disappeared behind a thick, suffocating blanket of darkness.

At these times, your loved one needs a Savior. At these times, you need a Savior. Remember, whatever Christ touches lives. If He touches your heart, your heart will live. If He touches the heart of your depressed loved one, his or her heart will live as well. If you reach your hand up, you will find that His hand is there, and in fact has always been there, waiting for you to grasp hold. If you hold tight to that hand, it will lift you up. "Then saith he to the man, Stretch forth thine hand. And he stretched it forth; and it was restored whole" (Matthew 12:13).

In your darkest hours, you may find that He is the only light; but you will also find that He is a never-failing light. If you choose not to rely upon Him, trust Him, and turn your fears and doubts and anguish over to Him, you, like Peter, will begin to sink. Even if you yourself are not depressed, you will begin to sink in despair and hopeless pessimism, convinced that the spouse, child, or friend you care so much about will never be able to change or to extricate themselves from the deep, dark pit in which their illness has trapped them. One of Christ's primary missions is to free those held captive by all forms of darkness that are endemic in mortality. He is able to free us from these bonds and to bear our burdens because He has overcome the effects of the Fall—including sickness, pain, and even death. "Behold, he changed their hearts; yea, he awakened them out of a deep sleep, and they awoke unto God. Behold, they were in the midst of darkness; nevertheless, their souls were illuminated by the light of the everlasting word" (Alma 5:7).

It is difficult—sometimes impossible—for someone suffering from the worst of depression to muster the hope that would allow him to reach out for the Savior. In such times, your faith, your focus on Jesus Christ, must be strong enough for both of you. The Lord will strengthen you and sustain you as you reach toward Him, all the while grasping the hand of your loved one.

The great Healer can mend *all* things, including the mind and body of one who suffers from depression. He understands all things, including the thoughts and feelings of someone in the darkest throes of this illness. You must be willing to turn all things over to the Savior. You cannot bear all things, but He can.

When many prayers for healing seem to have gone unanswered, you may be tempted to give up. It is then that you must remember that charity suffereth long. Charity doesn't give up, doesn't fade, doesn't pull back from abiding with someone during their darkest days. This is because charity is the pure love of Christ, His greatest power. And it is a power that He is willing to share with you. His infinite love and understanding come from His infinite suffering for the pains and infirmities and sicknesses He experienced personally through the Atonement. He has both felt and overcome the pain your loved one is feeling, as well as the anguish you feel. He has descended below all things so He can lift us above all things. His love is stronger than any sickness, any sin, any problem, any challenge.

To us, the Savior says, "I will encircle thee in the arms of my love" (D&C 6:20).

It is true that not all prayers for healing are answered in the time frame and in the way we would hope for. But if any man, woman, teenager, or child will allow himself or herself to be lifted in the arms of the Savior, he will be eternally saved in ways that are more important than anything that occurs in this mortal life. By faithfully placing your will on the altar and allowing the Savior's will to take precedence, you are not abandoning your loved one or ceasing to do that which you are capable of accomplishing through your own best efforts. You are adding His infinite powers to your mortal capabilities in order to nurture and comfort and save your loved one. One of His greatest titles is Savior because He can save anyone.

THE STRANGE PATH

How does one get to the celestial kingdom? I think most of us understand the big-picture answer to that question. We receive the saving ordinances of the gospel, obey the commandments, repent when we fall short, and endure to the end.

However, as we move beyond those vital but general requirements, the question remains: In day-to-day life, how do you move toward the celestial kingdom? What do you do when you get up in the morning if you want to reach that goal? What do you say to your depressed loved one when he tells you he feels horrible, when he says he doesn't feel like talking to you at all, or when he say he wants to die? How can you help him? What do you do in those moments?

On a smaller scale, the prerequisites needed to reach the celestial kingdom become much more personal, more individualized. Is sickness necessary? Is deep discouragement necessary? Is desperation necessary? How many prayers are required? At times, we may feel that heaven is close but never a short enough jump for us to arrive there. Mostly, as we live our daily lives, the way seems long and hard. Doubts may arise in our minds about where that road will really lead.

In the Book of Mormon, Alma prophetically tells the people of Gideon, "For I perceive that ye are in the paths of righteousness; I perceive that ye are in the path which leads to the kingdom of God" (Alma 7:19). On occasion, we will receive that same reassurance from the Spirit, and we will draw needed strength at those times. However, most of the time we must rely upon our faith in Christ and His Atonement as we walk the path of life.

We have each been placed on our own personal, sometimes strange path, and we must walk forward. We cannot leap over to another path that appears more pleasant. This is the path the Lord has given us, and we cannot choose another way to reach the kingdom of God. We can, however, have confidence that if we faithfully follow that path, it will lead us to the kingdom of God.

We can remember the story of Jonah. The Lord had a path for Jonah to follow. He said, "Arise, go to Nineveh, that great city, and cry against it; for their wickedness is come up before me" (Jonah 1:2).

Jonah, however, thought he saw a much better path, an easier path, and he started toward Tarshish. As we know, though, Jonah's plan did not get him to Tarshish.

After a brief but intense period of solitary contemplation, Jonah received another opportunity. "And the word of the Lord came unto Jonah the second time, saying, Arise, go unto Nineveh, that great city, and preach unto it the preaching that I bid thee. So Jonah arose, and went unto Nineveh, according to the word of the Lord" (Jonah 3:1–3).

The Lord knew what Jonah needed, and He knew where Jonah's path would lead him. We have a completely trustworthy Heavenly Father and Savior who have only our well-being and ultimate happiness in mind. Their work is "to bring to pass the immortality and eternal life" of you and me, and they are very good at their work (Moses 1:39).

Our only reliable road map, the one set out for us by the Lord, requires dependence upon "the merits, and mercy, and grace of the Holy Messiah, who layeth down his life according to the flesh, and taketh it again by the power of the Spirit, that he may bring to pass the resurrection of the dead, being the first that should rise" (2 Nephi 2:8). There is no alternative. If we try to use mortal wit and strength alone, we will fail. We must absolutely and completely rely upon the Savior and walk the path He places us on.

We must not be passive in this experience. We cannot sit by the side of life's trail and expect to go anywhere. However, if we have learned wisdom, we will be *submissive* in this experience. We will realize that our best—our only—way toward our goal and out of our afflictions, is to faithfully walk along the trail the Lord has laid out for us. We must actively move forward as fast as we can along that trail.

In Nephi 2:27, Lehi gives us our options: "Wherefore, men are free according to the flesh; and all things are given them which are expedient unto man. And they are free to choose liberty and eternal life, through the great Mediator of all men, or to choose captivity and death, according to the captivity and power of the devil."

You will note that Lehi doesn't say we are free to choose our trials or those of our family members. The One who knows the way to the celestial kingdom knows what trials will change and shape us enough to allow Him to take us there. We must be careful about running away from those requisite trials.

What can I say of myself after spending twenty-five years of my marriage at the side of a wonderful but severely depressed woman? I have changed for the better. I have changed in ways that I don't believe ever would have occurred without the terribly difficult experiences I shared with my wife and son. I have come to know God through our shared suffering. While I am certainly far from perfect, I am a more committed follower of Jesus Christ, because more times than I could ever count, I have felt His redeeming love supporting and strengthening me. He has never given up on G.G., me, or my son, and my love for Him has grown ever deeper. I know that I must follow Him.

However long and hard the road that leads me back to my heavenly home, I know that every step I take will be worth it. A time will come when I will look back on that road with clearer eyes and realize that it was a golden pathway.

PART FOUR
DELIVERANCE THROUGH THE ATONEMENT IS FOR EVERYONE

TEN

If the very jaws of hell shall gape open the mouth wide after thee
—D&C 122:7

The world is full of seemingly senseless heartbreak and sorrow. As Satan rages, it seems like the list of sorrows grows longer and longer: infidelity, divorce, abuse, same-gender attraction, murder, kidnapping, rape, SIDS, children going astray, unemployment, death or suicide of loved ones, ravaging disease, war, and countless other evil things.

It seems that every family is required to go through a deep trial of some sort—something difficult enough to try them as Abraham was tried when he was asked to sacrifice his only son, as Joseph Smith was tried in Liberty Jail, as the members of the Martin Handcart Company were tried as they crossed the plains in bitter winter.

Sometimes it seems even harder for us to bear the trials that our loved ones face than the trials we endure ourselves because we feel so helpless. Watching unmasked grief and pain is a soul-wrenching experience. Sometimes we forget that the Atonement applies directly to these occasions as well.

I am reminded of my friend Shannon Wilson, a BYU student who went to work in an orphanage in Romania. The place was an absolute sham. While the orphanage supposedly offered succor, it looked more like a dumping ground than a place of refuge. Children were dying of starvation and disease right and left. No one seemed to care. But Shannon did. She cared so much that her grief for these children cut deeply into her soul. *Why*, she wondered, *Why do these poor, helpless children have to suffer so much?* Then she received an answer I will never forget. She told me, "Suddenly I knew that because I was there, God was there." The peace she was seeking came into her soul, and love for the children poured from her. She comforted and loved them fully in their last hours on earth.

And so it is with each experience we go through in mortality. Where we are, God is also. If we seek the Savior, we will ever find Him, be it in our moments of joy or in our darkest hours. Our souls will find solace in His love and mercy and through the support of others who are striving to be like Him.

When Joseph was in Carthage Jail preparing for almost certain death, his soul was weary with the weight of the persecution he had carried since he was fourteen years old. What did he crave? The comfort of a song sung by a friend. A song he had long loved. "A Poor Wayfaring Man of Grief." Perhaps he needed its tender reminder that he was giving his life for the Savior.

A mother whose son was the brightest star in her firmament was told this son was valiantly fighting same sex attraction and had been for years. She was crushed and heartbroken. She couldn't imagine her son's pain and could not understand the unfairness of his affliction when he was such a valiant son of God. What did she need? To cry and be held by a woman of strong faith and testimony who could be relied upon to tell her that the world had not turned upside down and that the gospel was still true.

When the year-old baby of a newcomer to the ward died, the entire ward spent one weekend completely redecorating the mother's old fixer-upper house—painting, sanding, and wallpapering. To this particular woman, whose husband worked in Alaska, this meant the world.

An attorney offered free probate services to a widow whose husband had died leaving her very little, least of all money to pay an attorney. When her house was destroyed by a tornado, a contractor rebuilt it for free.

What do all these examples tell us? They remind us that although mortality is cruel, we can wring sweetness out of terrible trials if we hold fast and remember that the Savior has experienced every one of them. He will give us what we need—not always what we are expecting—but He will sustain us. We also learn that that sweetness comes through our fellow man. So often we are God's hands, voice, and ears. We are His embrace.

THE HORIZONTAL ASPECT OF THE ATONEMENT

When we feel the love of Christ fill our souls as we develop a personal (vertical) relationship with him, we naturally become consumed with a desire for everyone we know to have the opportunity to partake of this delicious fruit. We look around us and see pain everywhere. Like spiritual Mother Teresas, we long to heal once we have been healed. I have chosen to call this desire to reach out to others with our divine spark of Christ's redeeming love the *horizontal* aspect of the Atonement.

There are no insignificant acts of kindness. Each act of love is a tender mercy to someone, reminding them that the Lord is there, that they are not forgotten. As we grow in awareness of our Heavenly Father's grace and mercy toward us, we likewise grow in love for mankind. As we are healed, we become a bulwark for others who need our testimony, our example, and our healing touch.

During my depression, a dear friend brought me a picture of a weary woman struggling to scale a rocky incline. Standing on either side of her and grasping both her arms were women—transparent and outlined in white. They were her angels. My friend was my angel, and that picture has bonded me to her forever. Zion will be built by angels, and those angels will be Latter-day Saints who are pure in heart, who are able to make the bitter sweet, and who call down the powers of heaven on behalf of their loved ones.

When I think of Zion, I think of the Nephite civilization during the two-hundred year period after Christ's visit. Can you imagine what it must have been like to live in this time of incredible peace? I am certain there must have been pain. There must have been sorrow. But everyone had learned to fill their divine void with the love of God. And from this wellspring they sustained one another in every trial.

Being healed from clinical depression—or any other illness or affliction—does not mean you will never have another trial, but it does strengthen your faith and allow you to stand as a witness of the power of God for others. An understanding of the Atonement allows you to bless others' lives that have also been ravaged by grief. But we can only do so if we truly have a testimony of the Savior's love and atoning power for ourselves. And that kind of testimony is only born of affliction.

The question that lay in front of me when I became well was, now what? The Lord had healed me. I had a life. I could do things now that

I had never been able to do before. Suddenly, I felt consumed by a desire similar to Alma's when he wished he were an angel and could cry the Lord's redeeming grace to the whole world.

The horizontal aspect of the Atonement came naturally to me—in large part because of the afflictions I had suffered. I longed to share the Atonement with my brothers and sisters, to bring to them the sweet healing I had received, to help them change from the inside out.

I think of President Hinckley's response to the tragedy of September 11. The essence of his message was, "We live in troubled times. Now let's get to work" (as quoted in David A. Bednar, "Stand Ye in Holy Places," BYU-Idaho Address, 22 March 2002). When viewed in that light, all the tragedies in the world have a single solution—coming to Christ. And we can be a part of that solution as we help bring others to Him.

During my depression, I frequently found myself troubled by *weltschmerz*. *Weltschmerz* is a German word that means "world pain." I didn't want to live in this world of pain for one more moment. At one point, while I was writing a novel about World War I, I felt completely overwhelmed; the pain wrenched my heart. I couldn't imagine the pain of the world at a time when half a million people could be killed in one day (such as in the Battle of Verdun) for no discernible purpose. Trench warfare was hell on earth. In the novel, my character was suffering from shell shock, but because of the fear that he was a coward, he forced himself to go back to the front line, sacrificing himself there. My entire chest ached, and tears constantly brimmed behind my eyes. How could the wife of my hero possibly deal with the loss of her husband in this manner? I pictured myself as that woman. I was twenty years old and alone in a cold town house in Berlin with a mother-in-law who had just committed suicide at the news of her only son's death. I was practically catatonic with sorrow. Then, in my real life, as I bent over the dryer to take some clothes out, I clearly heard a voice inside me say, "G.G., you do not have to carry this load. There is only One who can carry it, and He already has. Because of His sacrifice, death is not the ultimate tragedy. The ultimate tragedy lies in not being who you were born to become."

My burden was lifted. The Savior had taken it. Now, as I am well, I still think of that experience often. Horrible things happen around us at every turn, and yet we can have hope for a better world through the Atonement. Our mission is to help change one heart at a time.

WHO WERE YOU BORN TO BECOME?

As I thought more about the second half of the revelation I had received—that the ultimate tragedy lay in not being who I was born to become—I began to wonder, who was I born to become? I got out my patriarchal blessing and reread it. There were some startling and very specific directions in it. I realized I needed to reach out in some way, and I began to think about writing again. Could I do it?

At about this time, Maurine Jensen Proctor, the editor of *Meridian* magazine, called me. I had previously been a columnist for the magazine, writing articles about genealogy, but I had stopped because of my depression. She wanted to know if I felt well enough to resume my work. I told her that the only thing I wanted to write about now was the Atonement. She said, "Fine—write monthly about the Atonement." And so I have. Sometimes more than monthly! Opportunities have presented themselves at every turn.

Then one day, not long after I began working again, I had a dim recollection of a sequel to a book I had begun writing some time in the nebulous past—a sequel to my previously published mysteries, *Cankered Roots* and *Of Deadly Descent*. When I got home that day, I asked my husband if we could search the old computer files for something to do with "Alex." (*Alex* was the heroine's name.) We looked around and, sure enough, there was a twelve-year-old file called "Alex3," and another called "Alex4." We had moved twice during those twelve years, and I didn't know how much of the files would even be intact. David tried to pull them up, but they were written with an outdated word-processing program. Being a computer guru, David, not without some difficulty, translated the files into something my computer could read. I pushed the PRINT button. Before I knew it, I was feeding the printer reams of paper. When the machine finally shut off, I held in my hands a complete mystery novel and the first three chapters of the next book in the series! I had absolutely no recollection of having written them. I had to read the completed novel through to the very end to find out who the bad guy was. It was an extremely odd experience.

Although the novel needed a lot of work, I was excited to begin writing again, and I could see that the story was set up to show how the Atonement heals families. I called my former editor, and she was very encouraging. So I went to work. I was a bit tentative at first—unsure of myself and my abilities, but to my amazement, after some intense work, my writing ability began to return. I didn't become a Tolstoy, to be sure, but I found that my writing had actually improved during my extended period of illness. It was such a joy to be using my talents again! That book eventually became *Tangled Roots,* and was published in May of 2007. It was shortly followed by another novel, *The Arthurian Omen,* published for a general audience, although it also discussed grace and redemption.

To my amazement, I found other unfinished works on the computer —all written during my years of distress and despair. And all waiting for the critical ingredient—an understanding of the Atonement. They are like abandoned children, and I can't wait to now raise them to maturity.

As I write, I find that my only desire is for the Lord to use me as an instrument so that others will be inspired to learn of and embrace the Atonement and perhaps gain some insight from my experiences. I've found that I am now better able to help others in my family, my ward, and in my children's group of friends because of my experience.

So how do you discover what it is *you* were born to do? Some people I know have founded an orphanage in Haiti. Some create inspiring and beautiful works of art. Others go to Mexico on a regular basis and build homes for the homeless. Most of the people I know bless and serve more quietly, but not one bit less importantly as they raise children, care for the sick, reach out in love to the lonely, and share the gospel. What is your talent, your mission?

We all begin our journey on a quest for our own salvation. We must come to understand the vertical aspect of the Atonement, our own individual relationship to the Savior. We must have a clear understanding and personal experience with the Savior and His Atonement so we can testify with power. As you build your own relationship with the Savior, you will then be able to take part in the horizontal aspect of the Atonement as you share your knowledge of the Savior with others and guide them to Him. There are four key elements that are crucial as you strive to understand and take part in both the vertical and horizontal aspects of the Atonement:

> 1. Pray. As you pray to the Lord, be specific as you ask
> for help to enable you to overcome the natural man

through His grace. The Lord will help you overcome all things, including temptation, discouragement, pain, doubt, and fear. Pray for a change of heart. Prayer should be a daily—and sometimes hourly—thing. Heavenly Father is ever anxious to hear from His children. Prayer in the temple can be especially effective, as well as prayerfully reading your patriarchal blessing. Pray to be shown your opportunities, talents, and abilities. Don't ever stop.

2. Study. In the appendix of this book you will find a list of readings that will help increase your understanding of the multifaceted doctrine of the Atonement. Although none of us can fully understand "the awful arithmetic of the Atonement" (Neal A. Maxwell, "Enduring Well," *Liahona,* April 1999, 10), the Lord can reveal to us through study what we need to know at different times in our lives. As we mature in the gospel, new understanding and insight will come to light, and our love for the Savior will grow until it fills our whole life. This is indeed a study for a lifetime.

3. Keep a Journal. As you pray and study, write about your feelings and inspirations. We have been counseled by prophets and apostles to write down our spiritual experiences that they may strengthen both us and our posterity. I like the way the author of a book called *The Artist's Way* puts it. The author claims that if we write three pages upon arising each morning, before we have even had a chance to have coherent thought, we will find our Creator and the creator within us (Julia Cameron, *The Artist's Way,* [New York: GP Putnam's Sons, 1992]). I have found this to be true. Amazing things are revealed to us in morning thoughts that are not yet jumbled by the events of the day. We have not yet had time to dress our thoughts the way they "ought" to be. They tell us where we really are. And out of them arises a wholeness of person. We no longer fear the

process of receiving inspiration; we are no longer afraid to dream. Through your writing, the Lord can reveal patterns to you in connection with reading and praying. The Lord will direct your life so that you are living it abundantly in service to Him. In the back of this book are journal trigger quotes from the scriptures and from the Brethren, provided for you to use as a tool in your personal study.

4. Attend the temple. Going to the house of the Lord allows you to experience, with Adam and Eve, the filling of the divine void. It also allows you to experience the intimacy of Christ's sacrifice for you individually. In a DVD entitled *Between Heaven and Earth,* President Boyd K. Packer reminds us that after Christ's crucifixion, the first thing to occur was that the veil of the temple was "rent in twain." I had always thought this was a symbol of Heavenly Father's displeasure at the crucifixion of His Son. But President Packer tells us that this was actually a symbol that Christ's sacrifice had breached the veil between heaven and earth. For the first time, mortal man was given a means of returning through the veil, back into the presence of his Heavenly Father. The veil of the temple is one of the most sacred places on earth.

In our Father's sacred house, we can receive revelation. We can pray, and we can experience miracles in our lives. We can bless the lives of loved ones who have passed beyond the veil. And by partaking of holy ordinances, we can literally walk in the footsteps of our Savior.

When you truly begin to comprehend the reality of the Atonement and allow its enabling power to transform your life—and share it with others—you will discover that indeed, this is the most important thing you were born to do. You will find yourself filled with greater peace and a greater sense of purpose that will light a fire in your soul. The

Atonement's power is the only solution to the troubles that plague individuals, families, countries, and the world. Working with all our might to bring this solution to others by using our unique gifts and talents is truly the work of a lifetime.

"For behold, this is my work and my glory—to bring to pass the immortality and eternal life of man" (Moses 1:39). When we embrace the horizontal aspect of the Atonement—by helping bring our brothers and sisters to their Savior, Christ's work becomes our work.

Through a greater understanding of the power of the Atonement in our lives, we can each experience our own divine deliverance and proclaim with Alma, "And oh, what joy, and what marvelous light I did behold, yea, my soul was filled with joy as exceeding as was my pain!" (Alma 36:20). When we begin to feel the joy and redemption that Alma speaks of in our lives, the Lord will reveal to us more truth, line upon line. He will show us how we can best serve Him, and He will help us as we strive to bring the good news of the Atonement to all of His children.

My life is not without challenge or difficulty. In mortality, we must press forward, ever climbing the steps to the throne of our Savior's grace. But He is our lifeline, our Deliverer—and that makes all the difference.

PART FIVE
PERSONAL STUDY OF
THE ATONEMENT

APPENDIX OF SUGGESTED READINGS ON THE ATONEMENT

SCRIPTURES: THE GREAT SERMONS ON THE ATONEMENT
2 Nephi 9 (Jacob)
Mosiah 3–5 (King Benjamin)
Mosiah 13–16 (Abinadi)
Alma 5 (Alma to the people of Zarahemla)
Alma 7 (Alma to the people of Gideon)
Alma 34 (Amulek)
Alma 36 (Alma to Helaman)
Alma 40 (Alma to Corianton)
The Letters of Paul

ARTICLES AND ADDRESSES FROM GENERAL AUTHORITIES
Bednar, David A. "In the Strength of the Lord," *Ensign,* November 2004.
Benson, Ezra Taft. "Redemption through Jesus Christ After All We Can Do," *Tambuli,* December 1988.
Christofferson, D. Todd. "Justification and Sanctification," *Ensign,* June 2001.
Cook, Gene R. "Receiving Divine Assistance through the Grace of the Lord," *Ensign,* May 1993.
———. "The Message: The Grace of the Lord," *New Era,* December 1988.
Eyring, Henry B. "Come Unto Christ," CES fireside address delivered at Brigham Young University, October 29, 1989.
Faust, James E. "The Atonement: Our Greatest Hope," *Ensign,* November 2001.

Hafen, Bruce C. "The Atonement: All for All," *Ensign,* May 2004.
————. "Beauty for Ashes: The Atonement of Jesus Christ,"
   Ensign, April 1997.
Holland, Jeffrey R. "Broken Things to Mend," *Ensign,* May 2006.
Packer, Boyd K. "The Mediator," *Ensign,* May 1977.

BOOKS
Callister, Tad R. *The Infinite Atonement.* Salt Lake City: Deseret
   Book, 2002.
Eyring, Henry B. *Because He First Loved Us.* Salt Lake City: Deseret
   Book, 2002.
Ferrell, James. *The Peacegiver: How Christ Offers to Heal Our Hearts
   and Homes.* Salt Lake City: Deseret Book, 2004.
Hafen, Bruce C. *The Broken Heart: Applying the Atonement to Life's
   Experiences.* Salt Lake City: Deseret Book, 1998.
————. *The Belonging Heart: The Atonement and Relationships with
   God and Family.* Salt Lake City, Deseret Book: 1994.
————. *The Believing Heart: Nourishing the Seed of Faith.* Salt Lake
   City: Deseret Book, 1990.
Millet, Robert L. *After All We Can Do . . . Grace Works.* Salt Lake
   City: Deseret Book, 2003.
Robinson, Stephen. *Believing Christ: The Parable of the Bicycle and
   Other Good News.* Salt Lake City: Deseret Book, 1993.
Skinner, Andrew C. *Gethsemane.* Salt Lake City: Deseret Book, 2002.

JOURNAL TRIGGERS

"And I have been supported under trials and troubles of every kind, yea, and in all manner of afflictions; yea, God has delivered me from prison, and from bonds, and from death; yea, and I do put my trust in him, and he will still deliver me." (Alma 36:27)

"Our understanding of the Atonement is hardly a shield against sorrow; rather, it is a rich source of strength to deal productively with the disappointments and heartbreaks that form the deliberate fabric of mortal life. The gospel was given us to heal our pain, not to prevent it." (Hafen, Bruce C., *The Broken Heart: Applying the Atonement to Life's Experiences*, 5)

"One of the great blessings that comes from the Atonement is that it heals those things that are unjust, those things that are not deserved and that we are not responsible for." (Scott, Richard G., *Church News*, 16 April 2005)

"Be faithful and diligent in keeping the commandments of God, and I will encircle thee in the arms of my love." (D&C 6:20)

"Look unto me in every thought; doubt not, fear not." (D&C 6:36)

"And he shall go forth, suffering pains and afflictions and temptations of every kind; and this that the word might be fulfilled which saith he will take upon him the pains and the sicknesses of his people." (Alma 7:11)

"And he will take upon him death, that he may loose the bands of death which bind his people; and he will take upon him their infirmities, that his bowels may be filled with mercy, according to the flesh, that he may know according to the flesh how to succor his people according to their infirmities." (Alma 7:12)

"The Son of God suffereth according to the flesh that he might take upon him the sins of his people, that he might blot out their transgressions according to the power of his deliverance." (Alma 7:13)

"But behold, the Lord hath redeemed my soul from hell; I have beheld his glory, and I am encircled about eternally in the arms of his love." (2 Nephi 1:15)

"Nevertheless, the Lord God showeth us our weakness that we may know that it is by his grace, and his great condescensions unto the children of men, that we have power to do these things." (Jacob 4:7)

"It is likewise through the grace of the Lord that individuals, through faith in the atonement of Jesus Christ and repentance of their sins, receive strength and assistance to do good works that they otherwise would not be able to maintain if left to their own means. This grace is an enabling power that allows men and women to lay hold on eternal life and exaltation after they have expended their own best efforts." (Bible Dictionary, 697)

"Thus, the enabling and strengthening aspect of the Atonement helps us to see and to do and to become good in ways that we could never recognize or accomplish with our limited mortal capacity." (Bednar, David A., "In the Strength of the Lord")

"Yea, I know that I am nothing; as to my strength I am weak; therefore I will not boast of myself, but I will boast of my God, for in his strength I can do all things; yea, behold, many mighty miracles we have wrought in this land, for which we will praise his name forever." (Alma 26:12)

"By the grace of God I am what I am." (1 Corinthians 15:10)

"And he said unto me, My grace is sufficient for thee: for my strength is made perfect in weakness. Most gladly therefore will I rather glory in my infirmities, that the power of Christ may rest upon me." (2 Corinthians 12:9)

"For by grace are ye saved through faith; and that not of yourselves: it is the gift of God." (Ephesians 2:8)

"Let us therefore come boldly unto the throne of grace, that we may obtain mercy, and find grace to help in time of need." (Hebrews 4:16)

"For we labor diligently to write, to persuade our children, and also our brethren, to believe in Christ, and to be reconciled to God; for we know that it is by grace we are saved, after all we can do." (2 Nephi 25:23)

"You can invite the Holy Ghost's companionship in your life. And you can know when he is there, and when he withdraws. And when he is your companion, you can have confidence that the Atonement is working in your life." (Eyring, Henry B., "Come Unto Christ")

"For behold, I, God, have suffered these things for all, that they might not suffer if they would repent; But if they would not repent they must suffer even as I; Which suffering caused myself, even God, the greatest of all, to tremble because of pain, and to bleed at every pore, and to suffer both body and spirit—and would that I might not drink the bitter cup, and shrink—Nevertheless, glory be to the Father, and I partook and finished my preparations unto the children of men." (D&C 19:16–19)

"By his grace, and by our faith in his atonement and repentance of our sins, we receive the strength to do the works necessary that we otherwise could not do by our own power. By his grace we receive an endowment of blessing and spiritual strength that may eventually lead us to eternal life if we endure to the end. By his grace we become more like his divine personality." (Ezra Taft Benson, "Redemption through Jesus Christ After All We Can Do")

"That urge to rise above yourself is a recognition of your need for the Atonement to work in your life, and your need to be sure that it is working. After all you can do, after all your effort, you need confidence that the Atonement is working for you and on you." (Henry B. Eyring, "Come Unto Christ")

"We need grace both to overcome sinful weeds and to grow divine flowers. We can do neither one fully by ourselves. But grace is not cheap. It is very expensive, even very *dear*. How much does this grace cost? Is it enough simply to believe in Christ? The man who found the pearl of great price gave 'all that he had' for it. If we desire 'all that [the] Father hath,' God asks *all that we have*. To qualify for such exquisite treasure, in whatever way is ours, we must give the way Christ gave—every drop He had: 'How exquisite you know not, yea, how hard to bear you know not.'" (Bruce C. Hafen, "The Atonement: All for All")

"So we must willingly give everything, because God Himself can't make us grow against our will and without our full participation. Yet even when we utterly spend ourselves, we lack the power to create the perfection only God can complete. Our *all* by itself is still only *almost* enough—until it is finished by the all of Him who is the 'finisher of our faith.' At that point, our imperfect but consecrated *almost* is enough.' (ibid.)

"Surely he hath borne our griefs, and carried our sorrows . . . he was wounded for our transgressions, he was bruised for our iniquities: the chastisement of our peace was upon him; and with his stripes we are healed." (Isaiah 53:4–5)

"Therefore being justified by faith, we have peace with God through our Lord Jesus Christ: By whom also we have access by faith into this grace." (Romans 5:1–2)

"How clear Christ's question was to a sinking Peter, after he had walked on the water: 'O thou of little faith, wherefore didst thou doubt?' (Matt. 14:31.) The moment Peter doubted and took his eyes off the Savior, he severed himself from the power of Jesus Christ that had sustained him on the water. How many times, likewise, as we have prayed for assistance or help with our problems, have we severed ourselves from the power of God because of doubt or fear, and thus could not obtain this enabling power of God?" (Gene R. Cook, "Receiving Divine Assistance through the Grace of the Lord," 79)

"God resisteth the proud, but giveth grace unto the humble." (James 4:6)

"And if men come unto me I will show unto them their weakness. I give unto men weakness that they may be humble; and my grace is sufficient for all men that humble themselves before me." (Ether 12:27)

"I can do all things through Christ which strengtheneth me." (Philippians 4:13)

"For if you keep my commandments you shall receive of his fulness, and be glorified in me as I am in the Father; therefore, I say unto you, you shall receive grace for grace." (D&C 93:20)

"If ye shall deny yourselves of all ungodliness, and love God with all your might, mind and strength, then is his grace sufficient for you, that by his grace ye may be perfect in Christ; . . . then are ye sanctified in Christ by the grace of God, through the shedding of the blood of Christ." (Moroni 10:32–33)

"On . . . the night of the greatest suffering the world has ever known or will ever know, he said, 'Peace I leave with you, my peace I give unto you. . . . Let not your heart be troubled, neither let it be afraid' (John 14:27). I submit to you that may be one of the Savior's commandments that is, even in the hearts of otherwise faithful Latter-day Saints, almost universally disobeyed; and yet I wonder whether our resistance to this invitation could be any more grievous to the Lord's merciful heart. I can tell you this as a parent: As concerned as I would be if somewhere in their lives one of my children were seriously troubled or unhappy or disobedient, nevertheless I would be infinitely more devastated if I felt that at such a time that child could not trust me to help, or should feel his or her interest were unimportant to me or unsafe in my care. In that same spirit, I am convinced that none of us can appreciate how deeply it wounds the loving heart of the Savior . . . when he finds that his people do not feel confident in his care or secure in his hands or trust in his commandments." (Jeffrey R. Holland, BYU Fireside address, 2 March 1997)

"And ye shall offer for a sacrifice unto me a broken heart and a contrite spirit. And whoso cometh unto me with a broken heart and a contrite spirit, him will I baptize with fire and with the Holy Ghost." (3 Nephi 9:20)

ABOUT THE AUTHORS

G.G. VANDAGRIFF is the writer who conceived this project because of her gratitude to her Heavenly Father and her Savior for the wonderful healing she received. She wishes to convey hope to all those who suffer from depression that healing is possible—even after twenty-five years of suffering. She is a graduate of Stanford University and received her master's degree from George Washington University. Previously she has worked as a college instructor, an international banker, and an assistant to the treasurer of Harvard University, but her great love is writing. She has published *Voices In Your Blood, Cankered Roots, Of Deadly Descent, Tangled Roots,* and *The Arthurian Omen.* She and her husband, David, now make their home in Provo. They have three children and one grandchild.

GREG VANDAGRIFF participated in this project because he was anxious to share the transformation that the Atonement and correct medications have made in his life. He was clinically depressed for his entire adolescence, and it was only during his mission that he finally received the correct medical treatment. He particularly wants to reach those youth who don't understand why they can't function at their best and who don't feel that they fit in—those who are unknowingly suffering profound depression. After filling an honorable mission in Atlanta, Georgia, he returned to BYU where he is studying business. He currently works part time for a computer peripherals company.

DAVID P. VANDAGRIFF joined the Church in Chicago when he was twenty-four. The first Latter-day Saint he ever met, G.G. Vandagriff, would become his wife and co-author of this book. G.G. encouraged David to write about the experience of being married to a depressed spouse and being the parent of a depressed child. David received his undergraduate degree from Northwestern University and graduated with honors from Pepperdine University School of Law. He has practiced law in California and Missouri and has worked as an executive in several technology companies. Visit David, G.G., and Greg at www.deliverance-depression.com.